THE LAST HAPPY OCCASION

THE LAST HAPPY OCCASION

Alan Shapiro

THE UNIVERSITY OF CHICAGO PRESS

Chicago & London

Among ALAN SHAPIRO'S many honors are a John
Simon Guggenheim Memorial Fellowship, two National
Endowment for the Arts Fellowships, and an individual Writer's
Award from the Lila Wallace–Reader's Digest Fund.
His most recent book of poetry, *Mixed Company,*
is also available from the University of Chicago Press.

The University of Chicago Press, Chicago 60637
The University of Chicago Press, Ltd., London
© 1996 by The University of Chicago
All rights reserved. Published 1996
Printed in the United States of America
05 04 03 02 01 00 99 98 97 96   1 2 3 4 5

ISBN: 0-226-75032-9 (cloth)

Library of Congress Cataloging-in-Publication Data
Shapiro, Alan, 1952–
    The last happy occasion / Alan Shapiro.
        p.   cm.
    Contents: Prologue—In awkward reverence—Woodstock puritan—
Come live with me—Fanatics—The last happy occasion—Sittin'
in a funeral place—Postscript.
    1. Shapiro, Alan, 1952–   —Biography.   2. Poets, American—20th
century—Biography.   3. Jews—United States—Biography.   I. Title.
PS3569.H338Z465   1996
811'.54—dc20
    [B]   96-14348
                                                                   CIP

⊗ The paper used in this publication meets the minimum requirements
of the American National Standard for Information Sciences—
Permanence of Paper for Printed Library Materials, ANSI Z39.48-1984.

This book is for my niece,

Gabrielle Barnes,

in memory of her mother,

Beth Shapiro.

CONTENTS

Acknowledgments

I gratefully acknowledge the Lila Wallace–Reader's Digest Fund for a Lila Wallace–Reader's Digest Award, which greatly aided in the writing of these essays.

I also want to thank the editors of the following magazines and journals in which these essays or versions of them first appeared: *Southwest Review* for "Fanatics"; *Threepenny Review* for "The Last Happy Occasion"; and *TriQuarterly* for "Woodstock Puritan." For permission to quote Janet Lewis's poem "A Lullaby" in full, I thank Ohio University Press/Swallow Press, Athens, Ohio.

Jeffrey Rubin-Dorsky and Morris Dickstein read the manuscript with care and intelligence; their advice and suggestions were much appreciated. I also want to thank Salena Krug, who, in copyediting the manuscript, made numerous suggestions that immeasurably improved the book. For encouragement, patience, and invaluable help with almost every page of every essay, I am especially indebted to David Ferry, Tom Sleigh, Robert Pinsky, C. K. Williams, Randolph Petilos, and, most of all, my wife, Della Pollock.

Prologue

On a short visit to Saint Louis in early February 1994,
I had dinner with the poets Jennifer Atkinson and Eric
Pankey. At some point in that long and very pleasant
evening, we began to talk about what we'd been reading
lately, and I mentioned that I'd just reread Eugenio Montale's essay "The Second Life of Art," and how taken I
was with his notion that the true life of art is not the
moment of its first reception, but the life it acquires in us
over time as we go from the music hall, the museum, or
the page back into the world from which the art itself

"took its first nourishment." Literary works and art in general, Montale says, attain their goal and achieve their form only as they circulate within our lives, in their obscure pilgrimage in memory and conscience, "mirroring themselves in that particular situation of life which made them possible." Isn't it, I asked my friends, an article of faith among those of us devoted to the study of literature that it's good to know a lot of stories and poems, that literature can change our lives, color our perceptions, alter the way we see and therefore act in the world? We pay lip service to the transformative power of art, but we almost never describe how and in what specific ways we ourselves have been transformed by the art we love. So I told Jennifer and Eric that I wanted to write a book about my own encounters with the second life of poetry, a book that moves continually back and forth between poetry and personal experience, examining as concretely as possible how certain poems taught me over time to read my own and other people's lives, and how those lives, in turn, have shaped my understanding of certain poems. Part autobiographical, part meditation, the book would trace the circulating current of that interaction.

Jennifer and Eric were interested in the project but they worried about the vaguely therapeutic, vaguely moralistic implications such a project might encourage, even despite my best intentions. I shared their worries. I certainly didn't want to write a poetry self-help book. The process of discovery I'm describing isn't always or entirely edifying. Poems don't necessarily make us better spouses, parents, citizens, or friends. The sorts of changes and transformations I have in mind are often morally ambiguous—sometimes beneficial, sometimes destructive, oftentimes a little bit of both. To enrich perception isn't necessarily to make perception more amenable to virtue, or to a particular moral code. Nor is it to make us any happier, for in heightening consciousness of what it means to be alive, poetry and art in general can overwhelm us with how brief, uncertain, and unredeemably painful life so often is. It brings us face to face with what so much else in our culture invites us to ignore: the inertia of our self-complacencies, our labyrinthine narcissisms, our penchant for self-deception, and most of all our utter vulnerability as mortal creatures in an unjust world. More often than not, what art insists we take a long hard look at is how limited its power is to save or console us in the face of extreme or terrible experience.

Much as Jennifer agreed, she herself couldn't say how or whether poetry had changed her life. Certainly the experience of reading particular poems had had emotional value, intrinsic pleasure. But what effects that may have had on the rest of life were too elusive to determine. I pressed her, asking, "But how would your life be different if you didn't know the poems you knew? Aren't there any poems you couldn't imagine yourself *not* knowing?"

That's when she began to talk about "At the Fishhouses," by Elizabeth Bishop, specifically about its closing lines, which she recited from memory:

I have seen it over and over, the same sea, the same,
slightly, indifferently swinging above the stones,
icily free above the stones,
above the stones and then the world.
If you should dip your hand in,
your wrist would ache immediately,
your bones would begin to ache and your hand would burn
as if the water were a transmutation of fire
that feeds on stones and burns with a dark gray flame.
If you tasted it, it would first taste bitter,
then briny, then surely burn your tongue.

It is like what we imagine knowledge to be:
dark, salt, clear, moving, utterly free,
drawn from the cold hard mouth
of the world, derived from the rocky breasts
forever, flowing and drawn, and since
our knowledge is historical, flowing, and flown.

Jennifer couldn't remember when she first read the poem but she had lived with it for so long that it was inextricably a part of who she was, as indivisibly joined to consciousness as skin is to the body. She said she almost couldn't wash her hands now without thinking of Bishop's icy, baptismal North Atlantic waters, without hallucinating that the water running through her fingers was a transmutation of fire, putting her in mind of knowledge ("what we imagine knowledge to be"), meaning time, mutability, the mysteries of conscious life in an unconscious universe. Because of Bishop's poem, even so mundane a gesture as washing hands became at times for Jennifer less a routine than a ritual, less a daily act of hygiene than a medium for contact with a heightened sense of life. If there was pleasure in her suddenly intense awareness of ultimate reality at her very fingertips, that awareness in turn was troubling and somewhat dangerous. It momentarily unsettled her familial comforts and stabilities by bringing her face to face with her mortality, with what is "flowing and flown."

Over the next eighteen months or so, as I wrote the essays that compose this book, as I revisited the sites in my own past where art and life had intersected in powerful and illuminating ways, Jennifer's story often would return to me and come to seem more true than either of us initially imagined.

Writing these essays, moreover, I discovered that for me art has a third life as well as a second. The third life is the life of public recollection that the essays themselves perform, a life embracing that first and second life but charged with all the needs, desires, and preoccupations of the present moment, and thereby altering the past the essays re-create. What Eliot says about tradition and individual talent is, I think, despite its limitation as literary theory, a suggestive metaphor for this dynamic interchange between past and present:

> The existing monuments form an ideal order among
> themselves, which is modified by the introduction of
> the new (the really new) work of art among them. The
> existing order is complete before the new work arrives;
> for order to persist after the supervention of novelty,

*Kuhn's paradigms
in The Structure
of Scientific
Revolutions*

the whole existing order must be, if ever so slightly,
altered; and so the relations, proportions, values of each
work of art toward the whole are readjusted; and this is
conformity between the old and the new.

If you substitute for Eliot's ideal order of existing monuments the sum of stories we tell about the past, and any
new transformative experience for the "supervention of
novelty," you have a fairly accurate description of the process by which the essays in this book were written. The
past, as I recall it at any given time, does form a kind of
ideal order, if by ideal one means the elimination of irrelevance, the selection and arrangement of a chaotic welter
of detail into a coherent story. As the present situation
changes, changing in turn my sense of what's important,
so too the past I feel compelled to write into the present
is altered "if ever so slightly" and recomposed.

Six years ago, I had no children. My sister was still
alive, she hadn't yet been diagnosed with cancer. My
father hadn't yet gone blind in one eye, his hands didn't
shake from Parkinson's disease. If I'd written this book
then, I'd have remembered many of the same events
much differently, just as six years from now, with new
and unforeseen "relations, proportions, values" to be

adjusted to the old, I'll no doubt have another kind of story to relate. In any event, the stories these essays tell about the near and distant past form a kind of palimpsest in reverse: the older images of myself are on the surface, revealing, in and through the way they cover, who it is who's writing this today.

In Awkward Reverence

On a Friday afternoon in September 1964, the day before
Rosh Hashanah, the Jewish New Year, some friends and
I, as soon as school let out, sneaked past the guards into
the Boston Armory to see the new cars of 1965. Large as
a football field, the main hall of the Armory was filled
with cars, each set up on a brightly lit mini-stage in front
of which an alluring woman in a low-cut sequined evening gown, microphone in hand, crooned to the milling
crowds about the features of each new model, answering
questions, inviting person after person to step up for a

closer look. I was still some years away from driving, but only months away from puberty, so even though I knew next to nothing about automobiles, the entire spectacle, women and cars together, had a dazzlingly erotic, if not exactly sexual, appeal.

Now when I see these same cars in old photographs and movies, how dated they seem, all the more dated for their touching certainty of being unsurpassably new, ahead of the curve. That afternoon, however, I marveled at the finless Grand Prix, the hexagon-shaped tail lamps of the new Ford Galaxie, the Barracuda's racy lines and curves, its wire wheels, the incomparable Mustang (the 1965 Car of the Year), the compact yet powerful GTO that the Beach Boys had just immortalized ("can't you hear it why-ya-ya-ine"). As I wandered through the showroom I thought that no earlier time could ever have been as fresh or exciting as the present moment. In my imagination of the world my parents found when they were my age, everything was black and white, grainy as newsreel footage, the cars all swollen and dowdy, old-fashioned even when new. If the term existed then, I would have thought that theirs was a world of clunky, artificial, and soon-to-be-superseded "lifestyles," whereas this world, my world, was sheer life itself, life at its most colorful and exhilarating.

In the celestial spotlights, on the green felt-covered stages, under the hands of those voluptuous women, the cars didn't simply embody dreams of speed and power. They manifested something much more general and vast, something like desire itself, desire unconstrained by any material limitation. From the cultural air I breathed, the cars seemed to draw down and concentrate on their shining surfaces all the vague inchoate dreams of *having* that all other cultural artifacts simultaneously aroused and failed to satisfy. As if they were the spirit of the new itself, possibility personified, immune to time, they represented an attainable unattainability. The cars gave off such incandescent freshness that it was impossible *not* to feel that owning one of them would be to live forever in the infatuating first pre-moment of possession, in a *having* made more intense for being incomplete, eternally about to happen.

I realize now, of course, that I was nowhere more the product of my middle-class, second-generation-American environment than in this uncritical hunger for the new. However much it may have made me susceptible to admen and merchandisers, there is something nonetheless about this hunger that I want to honor. The desire for the new, even if its focus is the latest model car, is a desire for renewal. And to feel renewed is to feel oneself made over, re-begun. Implicit in the body's pebbled sheen, in the whitewalls and grillwork, is the promise of a life pristine, immaculate, unmarred by time, a life of inexhaustible vitality. Okay, so we're all chumps, suckers, easy marks. The promise is never met, or never met for long. And each new thing we buy, unconsciously believing it will free us of ourselves, only confirms, sooner or later as the gloss wears off, that we are only who we've always been. Yet our American glorification of fads and fashions, the just-invented, the latest thing, isn't entirely the work of Madison Avenue. It is also an expression of a stubborn hopefulness of spirit. Like our founding fathers and the colonists preceding them, for whom the New World meant a liberation from inherited traditions, a shining city on a hill, our longing for the future derives in part from an inveterate nostalgia for beginnings.

Though we have largely desacralized our world and sacrificed the past to the promise of the future, there is something akin to religious longing in our hunger for regenerating change. According to Mircea Eliade, the rituals, ceremonies, and initiation rites in many traditional societies all speak on some level to this desire for rebirth. Through myth and ritual, what Eliade calls "religious man" symbolically effaces time, returning to the world as it was on the first day of creation, so he can feel himself reborn with his auroral vitality still intact. Such archaic hopes and expectations, it seems to me, still haunt the present. They hover about the rituals we devise to celebrate the new home, the newborn child, the new job, and even the new car. In my experience, they hover there more tangibly than they do in the temple.

The car show virtually coincided with the Jewish New Year, which, like all New Year celebrations, projects and tries to satisfy the human need for periodic regeneration. That's why the New Year is followed by a day of atonement, Yom Kippur, a day on which we purify ourselves of sin, cast out the accumulated imperfections of the past so as morally to make ourselves as new, as pure, as the coming year itself. That's what it is in theory, anyway. In practice, at least for me, it was another matter. The daylong observances, the hours of unintelligible prayers, the arcane rituals performed mechanically, unfeelingly, the endless rising and sitting, rising and sitting—far from abolishing time, the New Year services only crushingly prolonged it. So much so that I used to joke that if a doctor ever told me I had only a day to live, I'd want to spend that day in temple on Yom Kippur because the day would feel just like forever. No, the promise of regeneration wasn't in the temple. In the temple I was banished to the past, to an Old World of sheer irrelevance.

At the car show I experienced the sacred, or something like it. Profane time, time as the mere succession of irreversible moments, disappeared. I wandered, overawed all afternoon, from car to car in an eternal holy present, lost in fantasies (part James Bond, part Beach Boy) of hairpin turns on mountain highways, a woman (like the women now before me) admiringly at my side.

I forgot time that afternoon, but time had not forgotten me. When I left the Armory I was horrified to find that it was late, past sundown, Friday, Sabbath evening of the New Year. We were supposed to have eaten early and then gone on to the temple for the evening service. Jerked back into history, I knew my father would

be maniacal with rage and worry. But instead of daw-
dling, stalling the inevitable punishment—his stern voice
saying "Don't you ever again" as the leather belt rioted
on my rear end and thighs—I ran like mad, pulled like a
magnet to the very thing I feared so much I couldn't wait
to get it over with.

I took the most direct route home. Not down the
safe if roundabout main streets, but down the side streets
and back alleyways I knew less well and usually avoided.
As I cut through this or that backyard, I'd quicken
my pace, glimpsing in lighted windows scenes of families eating Sabbath meals, their peace and happiness
reminding me by contrast of what my own house held in
store.

I ran and ran, and almost didn't hear the lady call
me as I came up Babcock Street, still several blocks from
home. She was waving from the stoop of her apartment
building, her front door blocked by seven or eight bags
of groceries. "Sonny," she called, "yoo-hoo, Sonny,
please, could you help?" Her groceries, she explained,
had been delivered after sundown, and since it was the
Sabbath she couldn't touch them. Would I be so kind,
she asked, as to carry them upstairs for her?

Here was my excuse, I realized, my one-way
ticket out of trouble. It was a mitzvah, wasn't it, to help
someone in need. What a *mensch,* I could hear my parents saying when I explained why I was late. Such a
good boy. A saint. I lugged bag after bag upstairs to
her top-floor apartment, then down the long dimly lit
hallway, covered with pictures of children and grand-
children, to the little kitchen in the back. Over the
sink, the window looked out on the kitchen of an apartment facing hers. Two candles on the sill were flickering,
like miniature signal flares, to the two candles on the sill
across the alley. The silver candleholders had the shape of
slender yet intricately detailed leaves growing up around
each other, flowering in flame. They must have been
antiques. From the Old Country. In the dingy kitchen,
though, they were the only things that shone.

"If you don't mind," she said, now sitting at the
table where her dinner waited, "just a few things, Sonny,
could you put away?" As I unpacked the bags, she told
me that, young as I am, I couldn't appreciate America.
What a wonderful country. Then to prove her point she
told me about her childhood. Continually interrupting
her account to tell me where the groceries went, she

described how poor her family was back in Russia, in a
shtetl outside Kiev ("Oh the poverty, don't ask, you
never seen such poverty, the tuna in the pantry, please").
She reminisced about how dangerous it was, what with
the Cossacks, the pogroms ("the noodles go up there
next to the chickpeas"), and how her father ran away
when he was conscripted in the Russian army, and how
when he got settled in Boston ("No, not the bananas,
the bananas stay here on the table"), earning a good living as a butcher, thank God, may his soul rest in peace
("but the apples, the apples you can put in the icebox"),
he brought the rest of the family over.

  I half listened as I put her things away. It wasn't
that I wasn't interested—rather it was that I'd heard the
same tale, or versions of it, too many times from the
elders in my own family to quite believe it. It had no status as event, something that had ever happened in the
here-and-now, except as a story told to children so as to
make them more obedient and respectful to the elders
who told it. The tacit and sometimes not so tacit mes-
sage was, it seemed to me, Look how much we suffered
for your sake. How dare you not do everything that we
demand; how dare you not be the person we require.

When everything was put away, she walked me to the door. She said to come around again sometime next week and she would pay me, give me a little something for my trouble. I said that wouldn't be necessary. I wanted to keep the kindness as pure as possible, free of self-interest. By renouncing the money, I felt as if I'd socked away enough moral credit to keep my tone of voice convincing and sincere when I'd later tell my parents that I had found the woman lying on the street, her groceries scattered all around—thank God I came by when I did, who knows what could have happened?

"Thank you very much," she said. "The pleasure's all mine," I assured her. And as I turned to leave, she stopped me, suddenly looking troubled.

"Excuse me, Sonny, mind if I ask you something personal?"

"No, lady, go right ahead."

"You wouldn't be Jewish by any chance?"

"Well, yes, so happens I am."

Her countenance darkened. "Shame on you, Sonny," she said. "Shame on you," wagging her finger at me now. "You shouldn't do work on the Sabbath!"

I was amused and insulted. The nerve. The hypoc-

risy. For a moment I thought the humor in the unem-
bellished incident might more effectively pacify my
parents than the embellishments I was planning to
concoct. Fortunately, the moment passed. My parents
bought the story, whole hog, which, given what happened next, seems like an appropriate metaphor. The
next day on our way to temple, we ran into the rabbi,
and my father told him of the mitzvah I'd performed the
night before. The rabbi shook my hand and said I was a
blessing to us all. And that was that, I thought.

In temple, as always, I was bored and fidgety, unfa-
miliar to myself in tie and jacket. I hated dressing up in
general. I hated the expectation "good clothes" imposed
upon me to behave, to sit still, to act as formal as I
looked. So even if the red blazer with black piping on
the trim and collar had been brand new I would have
chafed against it. But it wasn't new. It was a hand-me-
down from my older brother. To add to the indignity, it
was still half a size too big. My mother, of course, as
always, told me I looked stunning, simply stunning. But
to everyone else it must have seemed that I'd mistaken
Rosh Hashanah for Halloween and come to temple
dressed as Captain Kangaroo.

Until the service started, nearest the altar, wearing the drab black suits they always wore, the older Jews in silence were already *davening*. Farther back where I was sitting, my parents and their friends and neighbors chatted amiably, exchanging compliments on the new suit, outfit, hairdo, shoes, or jewelry, as if the New Year were more fashion show than holy day. Then the interminable hour or so of prayers, of standing and sitting, my mind from time to time returning to the sky blue Sting Ray, the black Jaguar, the dark green MG, drifting in a half-sleep till I was suddenly awakened when my mother squeezed my arm, my father patted my shoulder. Before the entire congregation, the rabbi said my name. He praised me for my kindness and self-sacrifice. My having risked my parents' displeasure to help someone in need put him in mind of Abraham and Isaac, how Abraham in obedience to God was prepared to kill the son that God had brought him in his old age. Such adherence to the ideals of the faith was the essence of what we, as Jews, believe in. Everyone, he added, as we begin the New Year, ought to learn from my example. People were turning around to smile at me, at my parents who were nodding proudly, their eyes, their beaming faces, their every feature saying: our son the mensch, the Jew.

At the time, and for some years afterward, this incident came to typify for me everything I detested about the Judaism of my childhood. The ritual observances, renunciations, and restrictions that I was forced to follow seemed drained of any spiritual energy, divorced from whatever mystical experience they memorialized and presumably revived. To me, they were dead forms invented by dead people to be mechanically, superficially, and hypocritically followed by the living. The spiritual ideals of Judaism—loving-kindness, social justice, virtue and righteousness in all things—existed only in the margins of an otherwise secular American life; they existed only on the Sabbath, on the High Holidays, or in the temple. They never seemed to pass beyond the boundaries of the rituals themselves into the day-to-day world, the only place where they could really matter. The prayers, the dietary restrictions, the various rituals and customs, so far as I could see, never made anyone I knew less intolerant, less unjust, less petty or impatient. Nor did they make my elders less certain that the world they lived in, the "real" world of business, was dog-eat-dog, and in order to thrive there and provide for their families they would have to be as ruthless as they assumed everybody else was. Sealed off from life yet pretending to transform it, the exactions of religion seem to enable life to go on as it was, with all its tedium and unfairnesses intact.

My dislike of this hypocrisy, however, didn't necessarily proceed from any higher moral sense. I didn't want my parents to live a more orthodox existence, and didn't feel in myself any saintly inclinations. But the refusal of my elders to live more thoroughly the Judaism they espoused made it easier for me to think of Judaism as irrelevant to the life I was beginning to imagine for myself, and to chafe against even the relatively few restrictions it demanded. At the time, I wanted bodily pleasure and excitement, the beauty and grace and power embodied by the music I began to listen to, the girls I began to notice, the cars I fantasized about that Friday afternoon. Ironically, what gave shape and texture to the ideal bodily existence I desired were the commodities created by industries of culture, by the very world of business to which my relatives were primarily devoted. It was the "real" world they believed in six days a week that intensified the appetites that their religion would deny me on the seventh. My disaffections and desires were the pure product of a mixed inheritance—the traditions of the

Old World pulling unsuccessfully against the promised fulfillments of the New.

I only wanted to abandon the one and embrace the other. It was only later and, oddly enough, because of my evolving literary interests that I came to see the Judaism of my childhood as an inescapable part of who I am, and to think more deeply about the tensions in my Jewish American identity between spirit and body, past and present, old and new; between the powerful need for continuity and communal order, and the equally powerful need for regenerating change. Over the years, the more I read and wrote, the more I came to see in the poetry I studied and admired that tradition and individual talent were mutually entailing, not mutually exclusive. I began to sense a dim analogy between the social and religious forms of life and the forms of poetry. We no more invent the forms we live by than we do the forms we write by. The forms of life, like the forms of language, or more specifically the forms of poetry, are inherited and general—legacies the dead bequeath to us, for good or ill. Which is not to say these forms are fixed immutably. We modify our inheritance by necessity as we adapt it to the ever-changing contours of contemporary life. To live

well and to write well both require a continually impro-
vised negotiation and exchange between the irreducibly
particular circumstances of individual experience, and the
generality of forms by which that experience is organized
or in terms of which it's understood. Conflict between
the two is unavoidable: no social or literary convention
can do justice to the concrete textures of the lives we
lead, and no life is understandable or shareable apart from
those conventions. Out of this struggle, both are altered:
even in resistance, the self adapts, and is adapted to, the
conventions necessary for its intelligible expression; and
those conventions in turn are modified and renewed in
their struggle to accommodate new lives, new experiences.

"Church Going," by Philip Larkin, more than
any other poem, helped me bring these issues into focus
when I came across it sometime in my early twenties.
That a poem called "Church Going" could teach me
anything about my relationship to Judaism is no less
surprising than that a poet like Larkin, with his "Little
England" postwar jaded sensibility, could appeal to a
post–Woodstock American Jew.

What initially attracted me to Larkin as a tutelary

spirit had nothing to do with seeing in his notorious disaffection from religious faith an image of my own. I
simply loved the expressive music of his verse. I loved
the way in "Church Going" the iambic cadence continually changes from line to line, stanza to stanza, in relation
to the speaker's changing understanding of why he, an
unbeliever, still feels compelled to visit churches. In keeping with the tone of "bored, uninformed" irreverence,
the meter in the first two stanzas is so highly modulated
as to be almost indiscernible:

> Once I am sure there's nothing going on
> I step inside, letting the door thud shut.
> Another church: matting, seats, and stone,
> And little books; sprawlings of flowers, cut
> For Sunday, brownish now; some brass and stuff
> Up at the holy end; the small neat organ;
> And a tense, musty, unignorable silence,
> Brewed God knows how long. Hatless, I take off
> My cycle-clips in awkward reverence,
>
> Move forward, run my hand around the font.
> From where I stand, the roof looks almost new—
> Cleaned, or restored? Someone would know: I don't.
> Mounting the lectern, I peruse a few
> Hectoring large-scale verses, and pronounce

"Here endeth" much more loudly than I'd meant.
The echoes snigger briefly. Back at the door
I sign the book, donate an Irish sixpence,
Reflect the place was not worth stopping for.

The short phrases, the casual lists of things, the
constant enjambing and, as a result, the unemphatic
rhymes and shifting pauses within the lines, all suppress
without quite entirely destroying the formal dimensions
of the verse, so much so that the meter is barely audible
even in those lines with little or no metrical substitution
("For Sunday, brownish now; some brass and stuff"). The
speaker's emotional and intellectual distance from the
tenets of Christian faith is mirrored in the formal distance
between the demotic rhythms of the lines and the ideal
cadence those rhythms simultaneously solicit and avoid.

Over the course of the poem, the style by almost
imperceptible degrees is heightened. The bored irreverence gives way to first amused and then quite serious
meditation; the diction becomes less flatly descriptive,
more energetically discursive, and the rhythms more
emphatic. And in the last stanza, where he realizes the
extent to which he's still emotionally attached to what he
intellectually disbelieves, the clauses and lines now coin-

cide, the meter, the rhymes, the stanza itself—all of the heightening formal elements (the stylistic equivalents of positive belief) that before were muted by the speaker's comic skepticism—now stand out in very bold relief as that skepticism modulates into a kind of somber affirmation:

> A serious house on serious earth it is
> In whose blent air all our compulsions meet,
> Are recognised and robed as destinies.
> And that much never can be obsolete,
> Since someone will forever be surprising
> A hunger in himself to be more serious,
> And gravitating with it to this ground,
> Which, he once heard, was proper to grow wise in,
> If only that so many dead lie round.

Implicit in Larkin's disaffection and irreverence, his unwillingness to enter the church except when "nothing's going on," is more than a rejection of religious belief per se. It is also a distrust of social experience, a sense that his individual integrity can only be maintained in solitude, apart from others. This, I think, is a typically middle-class anxiety, one I thoroughly share. But the poem also comes to recognize that the collective identity is present nonetheless even when it appears to be denied: it's present in the very words he uses to deny it, in all the linguistic and poetic structures the poem utilizes, in the more than personal history those structures bear. So it's no surprise that the skeptical and solitary "I" would mutate into the corporate "our" and impersonal "someone" in the closing lines as Larkin acknowledges that all of us, as mortal creatures, hunger for some communal compensation for, or hedge against, the fact of personal extinction. Nor is it surprising that as this acknowledgment is made, those stylistic equivalents of a communal or traditional identity would speak more audibly through Larkin's solitary voice, making that voice less solitary if not less alone.

Wasn't this also partly the function of the rituals that old woman was so careful to perform? More than just the social puppetry they seemed to me back then, mechanical imitations of what everyone around her had always done, her observances, I came to realize, enabled her to ease to some degree what must have been a terrible isolation, a wrenching sense of dispossession. Where were her parents buried? Had her husband died? Had her children moved away, pursuing the opportunities only

Uncle Sam afforded ("Such a wonderful country!")? The silver candleholders must have shone not with a time-eclipsing novelty, returning her to some impossibly pristine primordial beginning, but with personal and collective history made vivid and immediate to her very senses. As she lit the candles and said the prayers her neighbors too were saying at that very moment, the fragile, evanescent moment would have been communally enlarged, resonant with other times, other presences. No less alone, she would have felt less isolated—at least for the duration of the ritual.

Looked at through the lens of Larkin's poem, even her hypocrisy began to seem admirable, a canny and resourceful form of self-assertion, as if the pressure to conform to all those laws, norms, conventions, to adjust personal need and desire to the communal order, had the paradoxical effect of enhancing personal expressiveness. In the interests of personal freedom I rebelled against the pressure to conform, while she and most of her contemporaries had to be more imaginative. In and through adherence to the code, they had to seek what freedom they could find. My friends and I were certainly more free, more uninhibited, maybe even happier, at least if you define happiness quantitatively, in terms of appetites consistently fulfilled. Whether we were more realized, or distinct, as individuals is another question. And this may be another way in which the forms of Jewish life (like all cultural forms) are similar to the virtues of poetic form: just as a metrical pattern increases the possibility of surprise (the more expected something is, the more significant and meaningful even the slightest departure from it has the chance of being), so also a culture full of ritual observances, of sharply articulated norms of expectation and behavior, seems to intensify and to make more vividly apparent the atypical, resistantly peculiar qualities of even the most passionate believer.

Eventually, though it took longer than I care to admit, I began to distrust if not my hunger for the new, then many of the objects I believed would satisfy that hunger. My enchantment with new things, my vulnerability to the hopeful glitz of even garish packaging has really not diminished. Even today, the heart incorrigibly quickens at the angelic aura of new cars on the showroom floor, at the neat racks of pants and shirts it is difficult to see and not believe that the body that wears them will be too ele-

gant ever to suffer. Wandering the radiant, nave-wide
aisles of Toys "R" Us in search of something for my
kids, I grow as eager as they do in the presence of so
much of what they want, and later just as disappointed
when nine-tenths of the pleasure vanishes as the flashy
action hero, the colorful Polly Pocket, is ripped from the
dream world of its glittery cellophane into the mundane
light of all their other toys.

This afternoon, I heard on the radio an advertise-
ment for a newly opened college hangout. The actor's
silky voice was promising such excitement it was sure, he
said, to leave me "screaming for more." A horrifying
promise when you think about it. Yet one that's truer
than the admen realize.

In my teens and twenties, "screaming for more"
would have been synonymous with heaven, for in those
days wanting itself comprised the better part of having.
Wanting itself was what had heightened life, imbued it
with such infinite possibility. Desire was vagrant, restless,
seeking only the ever-renewing promise of itself. Even to
hold it for a little while, each new thing had to seem as
free and limitless as the desire it would satisfy. It had to
dazzle by eliminating any trace of its historical existence.

The new cars in the main hall of the Armory gave no hint of the assembly line, of the hands that labored there, of strikes or layoffs. To solicit my desire, they had to stand outside of time, beyond the actual conditions that produced them. "Where can we take you? Who will you be there?" is all they ever asked, not "Where did we come from? How did we get here?"

It's the American side of my identity that heeds even today the former questions; the Jewish side, the latter. The one turns me nostalgically toward the future and its paradisal hope of new beginnings, where I, a kind of Huck Finn as consumer, am forever lighting out toward the Western Territories of the new and improved. The other turns me toward the old beginnings of the past, where my individual identity, my solitary mortal self, is extended back in time beyond the evanescent present by being joined to the dead in a kind of rear-view congregation. The problem is, however, that my allegiance to the one interferes with my allegiance to the other.

Together in my ear, each is the other's static. Much as I've come to respect the impulse for communal worship and yearn for the consolations I know ritual observances have brought to others, the promise of the

new, the fresh, the not-yet-tried, still makes me hesitate
before the temple door, and all that reaches me are just
the dead and unintelligible letters of the recited prayers,
not the living spirit. Like Larkin I enter only when I'm
"sure there's nothing going on inside." At the same time
I realize that nothing I buy or dream of buying, none of
the artifacts of contemporary culture, will ever shine as
durably as the Sabbath candleholders in that woman's
kitchen. Now when I see those delicate, thinly beaten,
eternally fresh leaves curling up around each other, like
silver flames themselves reaching toward the flames they
hold, each one distinct, yet indivisibly joined to all the
others, I see an image of the spirit world, in which solitude and communal order, the freshness of the present
and the stability of the past, consoling history and regenerating freedom, are necessary conditions of each other.
They represent a tangible ideal that I have never found in
the synagogue or in the marketplace, but only now and
then, and briefly, on the living page, in the attentive ear.

Woodstock Puritan

I

For some mysterious reason, most of my friends in childhood and adolescence were from broken homes. In grade school, the kids I ran with—Saul Chessler, Stevie Goldstein, Michael Carr, and Gary O'Brien—were raised by single mothers, and they all went wonderful places and did exotic things on the weekends when their fathers visited. They went to movies, ball games, circuses, museums; in the summertime, they took day trips to the Cape, or to the north shore; they went camping and hiking in Maine, Vermont, New Hampshire. I, whose parents were thoroughly, if not happily, married, never went anywhere. Whatever fission of the early sixties split apart the nuclear family inside other people's houses became the glummest fusion of the fifties in my own. And as the weekends rolled around and my friends deserted me, with my mother down in the basement doing laundry all afternoon, and my father napping in the den before the droning television, it was hard not to think that life was a perpetual party, and only those kids got invited whose parents were divorced. I used to beg my parents to please get divorced, or separate at least, so I could go someplace for once, do something exciting. They'd laugh and pat me on the head and say, "What a card, what a sense of humor."

By the time I went to high school, I'd long since given up any hope of their divorcing, but I was still drawn to kids from broken homes. My closest friend in those years was Jeff Morrison. At the beginning of our freshman year, Jeff had moved to Brookline with his mother and his brothers, John and Bruce, after his parents got divorced. Even at fifteen, Jeff was a handsome, even manly-looking kid, dark-haired and muscular. But his apparent manliness was qualified, if not entirely under-

cut, by his utter guilelessness, his incapacity for deceit or
dissimulation. He was kindhearted and too trusting. He
had an almost childlike faith in the goodness of other
people, assuming everyone accepted him on his own
terms as he accepted them on theirs. Though he never
talked about his family or how the divorce affected him,
I wonder now if his inveterate openness to others, his
almost reckless refusal to think that anyone would do
him harm, wasn't in some way a reaction to the pain and
betrayal he may have felt about his absent father, his broken home, as if he thought the more remote somebody
was to him, the more reliably familial that person was or
ought to be. Though it confused and bewildered him
when other kids would take advantage of his great good
nature, or when adults would misinterpret his naive honesty as disrespect, he was incapable of changing, of taking
on a more guarded, more circumspect demeanor. His
innate, unsophisticated decency seemed to prevent him
from learning from experience.

But it wasn't just his innocence that made him vulnerable to others. Jeff also had about him a rather hapless
air; he had a gift for getting himself into difficult and
embarrassing situations. I discovered this soon after we

met at tryouts for basketball. We both made the freshman team. The school supplied uniform and sneakers, but we had to purchase our own jockstraps. Jeff and I went to a local sporting-goods store. I bought a medium jockstrap. Jeff bought an extra large. Now I'd already seen him in the showers after tryouts, so I was a little surprised. He was well enough endowed, but an extra large? When I called him on this, he said, "Didn't you see that beautiful chick at the cash register?" I said yeah, I saw her. So what? "Well," he said, "I thought maybe if I got an extra large she might, you know, notice me." She didn't, of course, and now he was stuck with a jockstrap that maybe the Jolly Green Giant could have worn, but certainly not Jeff. It looked more like an oxygen mask than a jockstrap. All that year, as we got dressed for games and practices, Jeff had to put up with merciless teasing from his teammates. Invariably somebody would pull on the baggy cup and call down into it, "Anybody home?" "My man, you got room in there for all the team equipment," Dale Clark, one of the black kids, used to say. "You suffering some serious delusions." Jeff would laugh along with everybody else. He took the razzing in stride, submitted to it the way he submitted to life in general, with cheerful, even dignified acceptance.

Jeff was a good basketball player, serious on the court, hardworking, dogged, his face impassive, utterly without expression, whether he played well or poorly, whether his team won or lost. His interest and pleasure in the game seemed entirely intrinsic to the playing itself. He was intense without being competitive at all.

His attitude to the game couldn't have differed more from mine. By my freshman year, I was only just beginning to doubt my prospects for a career in professional basketball. In grade school I was something of a star. Physically and athletically, I bloomed early. In fact, I am now roughly the same height and weight I was when I was twelve years old, so back then I was bigger and more agile than almost everyone I played against. The men in my family, especially on my father's side, are rather tall. My father, himself a star in high school, used to tell me as I was growing up that I had big feet, I'd be taller than he was, and so if I only practiced hard enough, who knew with my big feet how good I'd get, how far I'd go. Unfortunately, while my peers continued growing, I was stuck at five foot eight, one hundred and fifty pounds. I went from power forward in sixth grade, to small forward in seventh, to big guard in eighth, and by high school I was just a point guard, and a rather small point guard at that. Even now, some thirty years later, whenever he sees me my father always shakes his head and says, "I can't understand it, Al, you had such big feet."

Anyway, being highly competitive and emotional, someone whose pleasure on the court depended much more than it should have on winning and excelling, I was drawn to Jeff's detached attachment to the sport. His single-minded, unworldly devotion to just playing became a sort of laid-back, unambitious earth to the ether of my intense ambition.

By the summer between my junior and senior years, however, Jeff's peculiarities took a political form. This was the summer of 1969. Over the past year or so, we'd seen the Tet Offensive, the escalation of the antiwar movement at home, the assassinations of Martin Luther King, Jr., and Bobby Kennedy, the Democratic National Convention in Chicago, and widespread rioting in many inner cities. It embarrasses me to say this now but I followed these events from a safe distance, with only casual interest. My two obsessions, basketball and my girlfriend, Martha (in that order, I'm afraid), were all I cared about. I had my sights monomaniacally set on my senior year,

when I would move into the starting lineup of the var-
sity team. But even if basketball hadn't so completely
occupied my mind and heart, I doubt I would have
joined the student-led antiwar movement. I was too
cowed by my father in those days, too fearful of doing
anything he'd disapprove of. Not that he was dictatorial
or hypercritical. Far from it. In his eyes, I could do no
wrong, especially as an athlete. If I had a bad game (and
he came to all of them, even hitchhiking sometimes out
to the remoter suburbs to see me play), it was the coach's
fault for not utilizing my abilities, or my teammates' for
not playing up to my level, or the officials' for favoring
the other team. No matter how I played, he praised me,
and the more he praised me, the more acutely I would
feel the discrepancy between the player he imagined me
to be and the player I knew I was. After a while I began
to feel his disappointment was in direct proportion to his
encouragement, his compliments a measure of my failure. The pressure of trying to justify his excessive faith in
my abilities made me resent him even as it terrified me
that I might let him down.

In reaction to the social turmoil taking place
around us, I think he began to fear that I might throw

away what I had worked so hard for. He grew more
watchful, protective, and authoritarian than he normally
was. We'd watch the nightly news at dinnertime, the latest body counts from Vietnam, the rioting at home, the
demonstrations, marches, drug busts, and even though
he was against the war, repeatedly he'd warn me that if I
got involved in any protests he'd disown me, as he had
already disowned my older sister. A graduate student at
Michigan State University, she was a member of SDS
and had been arrested several times for antiwar activities.
She was also living with a black man, her love life and
her politics seamlessly expressing an out-and-out assault
on the middle-class American values my parents represented. They'd already lost her, and they were going to
make damn sure, for my own good, that they didn't lose
me too. To keep me busy when I wasn't on the court,
my father got me a job downtown as a stock boy with a
novelty wholesaler. Mornings on our way to work, we'd
pass the hippies sleeping on the steps of the Arlington
Street Church. "Look at that," he'd say, pointing at the
long hair, bare feet, and dirty clothes. "If they want to
live like dogs we ought to treat 'em like dogs, we ought
to round 'em up and shoot 'em. How can they do this to
their parents?"

That summer Jeff let his hair grow long, partly to overthrow "the system," but mostly just to imitate his older brother, who, as I recall, was a rock musician and a poet. Jeff's relation to the counterculture (drugs included) was like his relation to basketball: it seemed to be based entirely in pleasure. To him it was, like everything else, just a trip, just what he was into. In the eyes of others, though, his ponytail meant only rebellion. To his teachers and his friends' parents, mine especially, he became a dangerous, subversive influence. It takes a certain effort of imagination now to appreciate the political valence dress and appearance had in those days. The sign with respect to hair and clothing hadn't yet so promiscuously separated from the signified. Of course, what started as a political statement expressing radical disaffection from the status quo became in no time nothing but a fashion statement that almost everyone was making no matter what the politics. By 1975, even my father wore bellbottoms, grew longer sideburns, and let his hair inch dangerously down a little over his ears. By 1979, in Skokie, Illinois, the adolescent neo-Nazis—who demonstrated for the right to march through Jewish neighborhoods in which many Holocaust survivors lived—all had long hair and scruffy beards, berets and earrings. They could have

been refugees from Woodstock, except that instead of a
red fist on their T-shirts they had swastikas, their earrings
sporting German crosses instead of emblems of peace
and love. In the late sixties, however, dress, appearance,
music, and drug of preference defined you quite precisely in relation to the status quo, politically as well as
culturally. So much so that, during the summer of 1969,
shortly before his trial for conspiracy at the Chicago
Democratic Convention, Abbie Hoffman could write, "I
want to be tried not because I support the National Liberation Front—which I do—but because I have long
hair. Not because I support the Black Liberation Movement, but because I smoke dope." As Godfrey Hodgson
remarks, Hoffman "was not saying that long hair and marijuana were more important than radical politics. He was
saying that they were, to him, inseparable."

Early in the summer, the basketball coach, Don
Slavin, asked me to round up a few other players who
might still be in town to participate in a clinic for grade
school coaches that he and some other high school
coaches were running out in Lexington. I went with Jeff,
Dale Clark, and I forget who else—there were five of us
in all from our team, and some thirty or forty kids from

other schools. We all sat together on one bank of stands, the coaches, some seventy or eighty of them, on another. Coach Slavin made some introductory remarks. Then he asked for volunteers to illustrate some particular play or exercise. Jeff was the first kid to jump down out of the stands. This must have been the first time Coach Slavin had seen Jeff since the spring. His jaw dropped when he saw Jeff's ponytail and red headband. "This is boy's basketball," he said with mock sincerity. "The girls don't meet till next week." Some of the players giggled. The coaches were all dead silent. Jeff didn't realize at first that he was being told to leave. He just stood there, stone-faced, waiting for the coach's instructions. "Go on," the coach shouted after a moment, "go on, get out of here. You're no longer on the team."

In his defense, let me say that Coach Slavin was a decent man, all things considered. Unlike most of the coaches I had had by then, he was too irritable to be a tyrant. He saw himself less as a Vince Lombardi "molder of character" than as an undeserving and long-suffering victim of the inadequacies of the adolescent players he was stuck with. During games or practices, he never chewed us out about our failures and mistakes. He never

ranted or abused us. Like a despairing husband with
a wife he knows he can neither change nor live without, he'd stroke his close-cropped head in exasperation,
pleading with us, whining, for God's sake, get back
on defense, don't rush your shots, look for the open
man. . . . Harried irritability was about as close as he ever
got to joy or passion. His dedication to coaching was
a function not of an overwhelming desire to win but
rather of a fear of losing, of humiliation. Not to be
embarrassed by us was his sole ambition. To play poorly,
of course, was one thing. To act badly, to show him up
before his colleagues, was unforgivable.

I sat there in mortified silence as Jeff walked out
of the gym. I was appalled and outraged, yet I knew that
if I did the right thing by walking out or speaking up on
his behalf I'd be thrown off the team as well. Even later,
when the coach pulled me aside to ask what in the world
was I thinking of, how could I bring Jeff here and embarrass him like that, embarrass the team, the school, I didn't
respond, afraid of what he'd do. I knew that by my
silence I had taken sides, and that it was the wrong side.
And I felt ashamed.

Jeff, on the other hand, didn't seem to mind.

"What a trip," was all he said when we met him later at the car. "What a trip," as if what happened was just what happened, something to contemplate with fascination or amusement. "Don't let him get away with this," I said, now angrier than ever, wanting him at least to stand up for himself since I was too afraid to. "He has no right to kick you off the team, it's unfair." But he just said to cool it, basketball just wasn't his thing anymore, coach did him a favor. I was amazed, admiring, and horrified at how easily Jeff could shrug it off, as if it were a superficial inconvenience. Basketball was inextricably part of who I was. Not to be a member of the team was as unthinkable as not to be a member of my family. The claim of both on my identity was so extreme that life without either would have been a moonwalk, weightless and insubstantial.

Still, I was too ashamed of what the incident revealed in me to let it go. That evening, after telling my parents what had happened, I surprised myself by saying I was going to quit the team. They must have known I wasn't serious because, normally, whenever I would announce an intention to do something they flatly disapproved of, my father would bang his fist down on the

table and yell, "Hell you are," and that would be the
end of that. But this time he just shook his head, sorry
for me, it almost seemed, as if he knew my self-righteous
indignation was a pitiful face-saving compensation for
my spinelessness. "Poor Jeff," he said, when I finished
ranting, "he just can't find himself."

Around midnight or so that night, Jeff rapped on
my window. "How 'bout a walk?" Well, if I couldn't
give up basketball for him, at least I could break curfew,
so I snuck out, and we went up to Cory Hill Park at the
top of Summit Avenue. For a while we sat in silence on
the small hillside overlooking the city. I wanted to apolo-
gize for being such a coward. "Jeff, ah, about today . . . ,"
I started to say, when he interrupted: "Hey, Al" (he was
holding out a joint), "let's celebrate, man, I'm free." I'd
never smoked dope before. I was a little scared of it, if
truth be told. Like all my friends, I ridiculed our elders
for believing that marijuana was the first step on the slip-
pery slope that led to heroin, but secretly I half-believed
it. I was, moreover, leery of anything, beer included, that
might interfere with basketball or jeopardize my standing
on the team. But despite my trepidations, I said, Sure,
yeah, far out, for Jeff, it seemed, was offering me redemp-
tion, a chance to make amends, to stand up with him,

take his side for once. As I took that first long toke I felt
giddy with the risk of it, with doing something I knew
would enrage my parents (not to mention what the
coach would think); I felt courageous, even principled,
like the kind of person I should've been that afternoon.

"Jeff," I said after a few minutes, "my dad says
your problem is you just can't find yourself."

"Your dad's a wise man, Al. A guru. I've looked
everywhere for me. I just don't seem to turn up."

"You ought to put out a missing persons."

"Yeah, maybe." After a moment he added, "What
do you think I'm doing, wherever I am?"

"Who knows. Balling a chick?"

"Who knows." Then he laughed. "Hey, maybe
my real self really is an extra large."

"No wonder he ditched you."

"Hope he isn't into basketball," he said.

"Why not?"

"Cause I got his jockstrap."

We laughed and laughed. I don't think I'd ever
laughed with such sheer abandon. The city lay before us
in a dense chaotic maze of glimmering lights. Sirens
crossed and crisscrossed on the edge of hearing, one now
fading away as another now came on, making my being

there with Jeff more pleasurable for the continual
reminder of what I had escaped. It was as if the sirens
were a citywide parental system of surveillance, sounding
an ineffectual all points alert that another kid had slipped
through its net of warnings, its constraints and hassles—
"Because I said so, that's why"; "Under my roof, you do
what I say"; "You walk through a field of shit, you're
gonna smell like shit." Another kid had slipped through
and entered a forbidden place where there was nothing
to live up to, or try for, and therefore nothing to fail at,
no one to disappoint.

I was only visiting that forbidden place, though,
whereas Jeff, it seemed, was settling in for good. As we
started back down Summit Avenue, I was already wor-
rying about how to get back into the house without
waking my parents, their imagined fury already closing
in around me, sobering me up, bringing me back to the
sullen law-and-order earth where I knew all along I had
to live. Jeff, on the other hand, was singing in a raspy
twang, his head thrown back:

> Then take me disappearin' through the smoke rings of my
>   mind
> Down the foggy ruins of time, far past the frozen leaves

The haunted, frightened trees out to the windy beach
Far from the twisted reach of crazy sorrow.

Yes, to dance beneath the diamond sky with one hand
    wavin' free
Silhouetted by the sea, circled by the circus sands
With all memory and fate driven deep beneath the waves
Let me forget about today until tomorrow.

How freely Jeff seemed to come and go. He didn't
need to sneak around, as I did, to find what little freedom he could behind his mother's back. He had no
curfew, no constraints, it seemed, of any kind. Out of my
own dissatisfaction, I imagined that his mother gave her
blessing to whatever he did or desired. She let him go his
own way happily, guiltlessly, without judgment or resistance. Under the chafing pressure of my father's love, I
couldn't recognize back then the almost orphaned loneliness implicit in his apparent equanimity, the "crazy
sorrow" that gave a less than peaceful tinge to his idea of
freedom. In this, I think, Jeff was typical of many of the
citizens of Woodstock Nation.

"Mr. Tambourine Man" was, in fact, the anthem
of the Aquarian Age. For the younger baby boomers,
those who came of age in the late sixties and early seven-

ties, that song marked the decisive turn away from radical politics to an almost exclusive preoccupation with states of consciousness. Though many rationalized this inward turn by claiming that all politics was personal, that you had to liberate the mind first before you could liberate society, the emphasis was nonetheless entirely on the self's interiority. That rationale, moreover, enabled many kids to justify, on political grounds, what they were doing for purely personal reasons. Now it was possible to get high, go to rock concerts, and "ball" to your heart's content and think you were doing your heroic part to overthrow "the system."

But the quasi-Eastern fascination with altered states of consciousness, with visionary dreams, with less restrictive, less "bourgeois" attitudes toward sex, love, and material possessions in general, wasn't merely self-indulgent, at least not in any conventional sense. This inward turn wasn't motivated by a rejection of societal norms felt to be too repressive, in the name of robust and uninhibited expression, so much as by a wholesale rejection of ways of being in the world that made one vulnerable to pain and loss. What we all craved, in varying degrees, wasn't freedom, exactly, but a sense of

belonging freed from the crazy sorrows, restrictions, and
ambivalences of the flawed and contentious suburbs we
had come from. We desired to replace our particular iden-
tities as individuals, as members of a certain family, class,
race, ethnicity, country, and religion, with a transcendent
self above and beyond the messy particularities of time
and place. We wanted to believe that what you truly
were you shared with others. What made them strangers
to you, and you to them, your personal history and
theirs, your ordinary consciousness with its unique and
unrepeatable lore of memory and desire, was really nothing but an inauthentic, because culturally constructed,
froth upon a sea of universal being that made us all just
one. And if we were all one, if everyone embodied that
single human essence equally, then we didn't need to
cling to those we loved. And not clinging meant we
couldn't hurt, betray, or disappoint each other. What the
counterculture offered in effect was not the liberation of
feeling, but a collective stoical retreat from all those habits of feeling, thought, and social affiliation that held
us hostage to a world that we could not control. Like
ancient Stoicism, the philosophy of free love purged of
Western possessiveness and guilt promised a state of mind

in which, as Charles Taylor describes the Stoic philosophy of Seneca, "the soul no longer touched by accidents of fortune is like the upper part of the universe, which rides serenely above the tempest-filled lower air."

Michael Lang, Woodstock's executive producer, had a similar vision of enlightenment while tripping on acid a year or so before the festival. Lang claims, in fact, that the idea for such a festival originated with this vision of an ideal nation, pictured as a many-tiered structure that is part wedding cake, part magic mountain, and part high-rise shopping mall:

> The first tier was the store with all the paraphernalia, nice karma, peaceful music. The second floor would have subtle changes, the sound and the texture maybe. The walls would begin to lose their shape, items that had a substantial feel would feel different on the next level. Everything would begin to shed its former skin as you climbed higher and higher. As you became accustomed to one experience, you'd want to seek the next. And by the time you got to the top, you were, in fact, free. Nirvana. A floating feeling and sounds, sensations, tastes—all free. A total environment. A nation away from war and racism, where drugs were easily accessible. With rock music and toys everywhere you turned.

The fascinating thing about this vision is the way it combines so many contradictory elements, blending together the traditional image of the spiritual quest as a mountain climb (think of Dante's *Purgatorio,* Donne's "Second Anniversary," or the allegorical mountain climb in part five of *The Waste Land*) with rank commercialism (the head shop on the first tier "with all the paraphernalia, nice karma, peaceful music"); political idealism with psychological regression ("A nation away from war and racism, where drugs were easily accessible . . . rock music and toys everywhere you turned"). The higher you go into this spiritual emporium the less distinct everything becomes. Just as "items"—the mercantile connotations are probably not accidental—shed their skin and dissolve into an indefinite haze, so your own identity (with all its imperfection and ambivalence) dissolves into pure, disembodied feelings, sensations, a floating sentient fetal-like amorphousness. If there's no war or racism in such a nation that's because there's no history, which is to say, no people, no individuals with differing and therefore possibly conflicting interests, needs, aspirations.

Yet to reach that Edenic toy store of effortless fulfillment you have to climb. Implicit in the image of an upward quest (even if it's on an escalator) is the recognition of some degree of effort, struggle, even self-denial. For those who took it to its logical extreme, the ideal of free love, peace, and harmony through sexual liberation, drugs, and rock music proved every bit as rigorous and severe in its demands as even the most ascetic practices. Some years later, I remember Jeff excoriating himself for feeling jealous at a party when he looked up while "balling" a girl he didn't know and saw the girl he'd come with "balling" another guy. Jealousy may be, as he believed, "a bourgeois fiction," but we were products of the bourgeoisie, and it took terrific effort to extirpate its values and assumptions from the mind. In the same paradoxical way that the doctrine of predestination enabled the New England Puritan to call upon almost superhuman reserves of will and ingenuity in meeting the challenges of the New World, the guilt-free ethic of the Aquarian Age produced extraordinary guilt in those who tried to live by it. Perhaps the flower children were nowhere more American than in the puritanical anxiety with which they went about cleansing their hearts and souls of their own past, in the merciless demands they imposed upon themselves to get beyond a culture of demand, self-denial, and guilt.

In saying all of this I don't mean to bash the
sixties. Nor do I want to make a virtue of my own
deficiencies and claim or imply that my hesitation to
follow Jeff into the world he was beginning to enter
proceeded from any sort of strength of character, from a
capacity to deal unflinchingly with what he and many
like him seemed eager to escape. At the time, I saw the
counterculture only as a sexual and psychedelic paradise I
yearned to enter with hormonally driven desperation,
but was simply too afraid to, attached as I still was to my
father's love, to the ordinary, angst-ridden, ambivalent
relations that nonetheless, with bracing clarity as well as
pain, reminded me of who I was. If the euphoria and
freedom Jeff pursued turned out to be self-destructive in
certain ways, my fear of that freedom and euphoria, if
not so self-destructive, was certainly less fun.

However naive or deluded, however much it was,
for many, just a flimsy cloak for other darker things,
there's still much to admire in the counterculture's vision
of a more cooperative, less acquisitive, less ego-centered
way of living in the world. To realize that an understandable disaffection with the status quo, with ordinary life at
a particular time and place, became for many of the
young a disaffection with life itself, with life as it could

be lived by anyone at any time, is not to deny the valid-
ity of such countercultural ideals as benevolence and
generosity, openness and trust. For all their impracticality,
these ideals still serve as an important measure of the pos-
sibilities of being, which life now, as we ordinarily live it,
has perhaps too easily forgotten or suppressed.

II

In any event, I didn't begin to sort through my conflicting attitudes about the period until a good decade later
while studying Thom Gunn's poetry of the sixties and
seventies. That a poem such as "The Geysers" should
have helped me understand the darker side of liberation
was ironic, for this poem, like so many of Gunn's poems
about sex and drugs, is a celebration, not a critique, of
the counterculture's Dionysian excesses. Gunn's passionate affirmation of these years was something I needed to
hear; even now, it forces me to qualify my own suspicion
and ambivalence. In his autobiographical essay, "My Life
up to Now," he describes the period as "the fullest years
of my life, crowded with discovery both inner and outer,
as we moved [with the aid of sexual promiscuity and
LSD] between ecstasy and understanding." However

quickly that euphoria faded into something far less inno-
cent, he refuses to deny "the vision of what the world
might be like. Everything that we glimpsed—the trust,
the brotherhood, the repossession of innocence, the
nakedness of spirit—is still a possibility and will continue
to be so."

Knowing now how dangerous that euphoric
vision turned out to be for Jeff, whenever I consider
Gunn's more celebratory and moving account of what
went on in those days, I have to remind myself how
different his situation was from ours, or from that of the
majority of Americans who eagerly experimented with
alternative ways of living. Even aside from his homosexu-
ality, as an Englishman living in San Francisco whose
parents were already dead, and whose relatives lived far
away, he had a kind of freedom and independence that
many of us, still caught up in those parental dramas of
rebellion, sorely lacked. Already in his forties by the early
seventies, Gunn was much older than we were. He was,
moreover, a highly respected poet, teaching at Berkeley.
He had a firmly established and publicly acknowledged
sense of self unavailable to me or Jeff. Our relative lack of
experience may have made us flexible and open to the

counterculture's paradisal dream, but it also made us
more uncritically accepting, less discriminating. To those
like Jeff, that dream invited not the freedom of a fuller
life but the freedom to evade, and therefore never overcome, the insecurities and ambiguities most middle-
class adolescents of our generation had to face. That
evasion, for him and many like him, had devastating
consequences.

"The Geysers" crystallized for me both the incred-
ible beauty of those years and the dangers that were
inextricably bound up with that beauty, both the positive
and negative motivations involved in the pursuit of it. It
is a poem about transcendence of the ordinary conditions
of human life through what Gunn in the essay quoted
earlier calls "hedonistic and communal love." The transcendence is simultaneously upward and downward:
upward toward a kind of godlike freedom from
constraints and limitations, and downward toward a
preconscious, even preanimate oneness with the natural
world. The men and women, heterosexuals and homosex-
uals, who camp here in the prelapsarian world of the
geysers are all naked, their nakedness itself a figure for
their desire to divest themselves of custom, memory, of

all the accoutrements of ordinary life that define them as individuals. Stripped down to an almost undifferentiated being, they are described first as "talking animals," and then "like plants and birds," filling out this unclaimed space "without too many words / Treating of other places they have been." All of the images in the first two sections of the poem not only foreshadow the more-than-human, less-than-human state the speaker will achieve in the sexual orgy of the concluding part; they also indirectly picture what it is about the human condition he desires to escape: the two birds that "like one dart upstream toward the falls," and the snake "alert in its skin" that "does not watch itself," living by sheer instinct alone, are immersed in the present, at one with their surroundings. They have a wholeness and indivisibility denied to us. This is what Keats means when he calls the nightingale immortal ("Thou wast not made for Death, Immortal Bird"), for, being at one with the eternal holy present, the nightingale is unaware of death. Unlike the human speaker, who suffers from his consciousness of time, of loss, of his neediness and vulnerability, the nightingale can neither mourn the past nor fearfully anticipate the future. Here among the cool streams of this natural

setting the talking animals approximate that preconscious
state:

> Some rest and pass a joint, some climb the fall:
> Tan, black and pink, firm shining bodies, all
> Move with a special unconsidered grace.
> For though we have invaded this glittering place
> And broke the silences, yet we submit:
> So wholly, that we are details of it.

But the racial and sexual harmony pictured here takes a
darker turn in the next section as the speaker, alone,
climbs from the cool stream to the geysers. Like Michael
Lang's vision of an ideal nation, the transcendent vision
afforded by the geysers also involves a climb. But the
landscape one ascends to, unlike Lang's, almost alle-
gorically embodies the human cost of such a radical
transcendence to one's prehuman source:

> A cinderfield that lacks all skin of soil,
> It has no complication, no detail,
> The force too simple and big to comprehend,
> Like a beginning, also like an end.
> No customs I have learned can make me wise
> To deal with such. And I do recognize
> —For what such recognition may be worth—

> Fire at my centre, burning since my birth
> Under the pleasant flesh. Force calls to force.
> Up here a man might shrivel in his source.

Reaching the geyser, the speaker has gone beyond whatever he has learned from custom or past experience. This landscape, unlike the more accommodating one below, has no complication, no detail, no familiar markers by which he might distinguish good from bad, beginning from end. The radical transcendence it offers is not the free-floating Nirvana Michael Lang imagines, but a deeply ambiguous, amoral source that is simultaneously outside the self and inside it. Here the self with its own complications and details, its history, its habits and desires, is burned down to an impersonal force, "under the pleasant flesh."

The bathhouse section that concludes the poem draws away, it seems, from such austere impersonality. The bathhouse appears to be situated somewhere between the Edenic harmony of the cool stream and the solitary and stringently burning source of the geysers. If "a man might shrivel in his source" up there, here in the hot bath he can move at one and the same time down through the self toward some prehuman origin, and out

toward others in a communal embrace. The boundaries
of the ego, of self and other, male and female, human
and nonhuman, dissolve as the speaker goes from not
knowing who is who, "not certain who I am or where,"
to a kind of reptilian passivity "plated slow / stretching
my coils on coils," to a kind of fetal, oceanic oneness
with the scene ("and bobbing in the womb, all round me
Mother / I am part of all there is no other . . ."). What
Gunn describes here is not dissimilar from Lang's Nirvana. In both visions, freedom from the human has a
strong regressive element; it means returning to or rees-
tablishing an embryonic unity in which all the doublings
that consciousness entails, the painful divisions within the
self between mind and body, and between the self and
others and the external world in general, are healed.
Whether this unity involves, as Gunn suggests, a diffu-
sion of the self into the world, or a contraction of the
world into the self, whether it's pantheistic or solipsistic,
seems beside the point. What's crucial is that, in either
case, there are no others, and if there are no others to
acknowledge or attend to in any ordinary sense, then
there is no risk, no neediness, no possibility of loss.
Gunn indicates the power of this regressive urge by

describing the appearance of other people in the subse-
quent passage as a painful rebirth: "It tore / what flash
cut / made me fugitive / caesarean lightning lopped me
off separate. . . ." It's as if the speaker has reversed his biological (and evolutionary) history and returned to the
womb of Mother Earth in order to be born again into a
world of others, where in their sexual orgy they can reestablish that primal unity, but on a higher level:

> I brace myself light strong and clear
> and understand why I came here
>
> entering their purpose as they enter mine
> I am part of all
>   hands take
>   hands tear and twine
>
> I yielded
>   oh, the yield
>   what have I slept?
> my blood is yours   the hands that take accept
>
>   •   •   •
>
> torn from the self
>   in which I breathed and trod
> I am
>   I am raw meat
>   I am a god

The Dionysian ecstasy of the experience, as beautiful as it is terrifying, is undeniable. But what is also undeniable, it seems to me, is that to be a god or meat—pure spirit freed of bodily limitation, or pure body unburdened of mind—is no longer to be human. Both extremes eliminate the very qualities that define us as creatures of consciousness and choice, dependent on and therefore always at the mercy of a world we can't control. Both extremes eliminate the historical dimension from experience: a god has no history because he cannot change or die; and pure animal consciousness has no history either because, living entirely by instinct, it cannot recollect the distant past or anticipate the distant future ("Let me forget about today until tomorrow"). To be one or the other, to be simplified into divine or animal completeness, is no longer to be human, and that of course is precisely its appeal. This is not to say that the utopian dimension of such ecstasy, the glimpse it offers of communal love, is deluded or false. Nor is it to say that an ideal is wrong just because it can have dangerous or destructive consequences for those who try to live by it (think of the inhuman slaughter committed in the name of Judeo-Christian values, or in the name of love of

country, or democracy). Kids like Jeff who sought to live
forever in that hedonistic freedom, not merely glimpse
it on a weekend holiday, were motivated less by that utopian dream than by a desire to escape the risk-laden,
needy incompleteness of human life itself.

Of course to be a god or meat is also not to be a
poet. To be a poet is to heighten the very qualities—
keen awareness, memory, a historical sensitivity to words
and rhythms—that either extreme destroys. One of the
most interesting aspects of "The Geysers" is Gunn's decision to write about such an expansive and indefinite
experience in the tightest, most definite of forms—
iambic pentameter couplets. This decision is more than
a rhetorical strategy to convey the infinite through the
finite, the unstructured through the structured. For the
strategy itself represents an allegiance to a complicated
sense of life contradicted by the very experience he's
affirming. What I learned from the poem when I first
came across it in the late seventies as an aspiring poet
were the very things that made me distrust the experience that the poem celebrates. The poem taught me that,
as an artist, as a technician of awareness, of keen perception, immersed in language, in the transpersonal history

that language bears, one is always doubled, always standing to some extent outside of what one writes about,
even when one writes about the purity of absolute possession. The speaker of "The Geysers" desires to transform
the complicated inside/outside relation to his own experience into the "unconsidered grace" of animal or divine
completeness. But the person implied by the poem itself,
by the subtle and ironic control implicit in the form, is
never wholly possessed. As a man, Gunn may be tempted
to dissolve into a part of consciousness, but as an artist he
remains committed to the whole of it.

III

Much to my surprise, my father didn't threaten to disown
me, didn't rant and rave, when I told him Jeff and I were
going to go to Woodstock. By that point in the summer,
he was too worried about me to make much of a scene,
afraid perhaps that if he put his foot down he might lose
me as he had my sister. I still dutifully went to work each
day. I still played ball in various summer leagues in the
evening. I worked hard studying for my SATs so I could
get into a Division III school (meaning academically
challenging) where I'd have a chance of playing college
ball. But I did all this in silent protest, asserting my inde-

pendence by doing glumly, sulkily, all that he demanded
of me. By withdrawing from him, I rebelled against his
power even as I submitted to it. Whenever I was home, I
stayed in my room and read or studied or listened to the
records Jeff would lend me. Late at night, I was also
sneaking out with Jeff to Cory Hill Park, where we'd get
high and talk and sing. Despite the mainstream's warnings of the evils of dope, I was still no less committed to
my various ambitions. Without diminishing my obsessive
drive, the dope provided a marvelous relief from it, a
temporary space in which I could just be, just enjoy myself with no thought of winning or losing anyone's
approval. It was on one of these nights that Jeff told
me that his brother had scored a couple of extra tickets
to the festival and that Jeff and I could have them. I imagined a festival full of Jeffs, of kids like him, free spirits
getting high, balling, dancing to the music we loved. It
would be the adolescent version of the party that all of
my childhood friends had gotten to go to, a festival of
kids from broken homes. Now it would be my chance
to go.

 "What about basketball?" my father pleaded.
"School? College?"

 "What about them?"

"Once you're up there with those hippies, that'll be the end of that. Believe me. I'm telling you, you won't come back."

He seemed more sad than angry, his sadness a mixture of befuddlement and defeat, as if his only hope now of holding on to me were to let me go. In me at that moment I think he saw the ironic fruits of a grimly virtuous existence, of a lifetime of denial and self-sacrifice in the name of making life easier for his children. I don't think my father ever held a job he loved, or ever expected to. Whether he was serving as the foreman in his father's slaughterhouse, or running the belt manufacturing business that his brother owned, or, as now in 1969, a salesman in the men's department of Saks, work always and only meant the antithesis of pleasure, self-expression, and fulfillment—the flower child's holy trinity. Work was what you did for money, and money in turn was what you laid away, first for your children's education, and then for your retirement so you wouldn't have to be dependent on your children in your old age. This dedication to our welfare he never lorded over us. The dedication was simply how a man, a father, was supposed to live. If you expected a medal for acting like a mensch, then you were definitely not a mensch. What he expected of me was respect, by which he meant conformity to how a man should live.

I don't think either of us realized that afternoon, as we sat across the kitchen table from each other, that my generation's utopian expectations for a life of play and freedom were created by the very material comforts his generation worked so hard to give us. When I think now of all the pleasures we regarded as our birthright, the moral constraints and inhibitions that had defined his life, and that we cast aside, to quote Philip Larkin, like "an outdated combine harvester," I imagine that there must have been some element of envy in his disapproval. He may have glimpsed in our rebellion an image of freedom he secretly desired. And glimpsing this, he may have felt like an unacknowledged and embittered Moses, watching his children crossing over to the very promised land to which he'd led them, but was too old himself to enter.

Max Yasgur's farm did seem like the promised land to me and Jeff when we arrived that Thursday afternoon, a day before the festival officially began. Jeff's brother told us Woodstock would be one gigantic communal happening, so we didn't need to bring anything

with us but a sleeping bag. When we got to the camp-
grounds, he and his girlfriend set up their tent, laid a few
joints on us, then sent us on our way.

By that time there were already some sixty thousand kids scattered across the fifty-acre farm. We found
our way to an area called Hog Farm, named after a commune based in New Mexico, a hundred of whose
members had been flown in by the festival organizers to
help with crowd control. These were career hippies, the
freaks of the freaks, wholly dedicated to communal living
and enlightenment through dope, acid, and organic food.
They had set up a free kitchen for those who had come
without money, and various first-aid tents for kids on
bad trips or overdoses. There was a small stage there as
well, where lesser-known groups performed for those
who couldn't get to the main concert. Everyone was very
friendly in a cosmic, dreamy sort of way, some of the
men in dresses, pajama bottoms, buckskin trousers, vests
patched together with pieces of the American flag, the
women in long peasant skirts, some in Day-Glo halter
tops, some bare-breasted, with naked babies in their
arms. One guy in a white toga, sandals, and top hat
walked past us saying over and over to himself, as if it
were a mantra, "I peak therefore I freak."

As a city kid who'd never had so much as an out-
ing in the country, I was utterly taken by the pastoral
setting, the wide fields sloping into one another, the
green ponds, the patches of woods, and the blue sky overhead as deep and clear as it must have looked on the first
day of creation. There were no police, no authorities,
it seemed, of any kind. Here we could do openly with
no fear of reprisal what we had grown accustomed to
doing late at night behind locked doors. Wherever we
happened to be, at any time, without anxiety or circumspection, whenever we wanted, we could get high or ball
our brains out if the opportunity arose. Truly, it seemed,
we had entered a new world that stood on its head
the values and mores of the old one. Maybe my father
was right. Maybe I wouldn't return.

Late in the day, we came upon a large pond where
thirty or so kids were skinny-dipping. Without hesitat-
ing, Jeff took his clothes off and joined them. I hung
back. I was deeply self-conscious about my body. Even
to take a shower in the privacy of my own bathroom I
had to overcome some degree of inhibition. And even
though my girlfriend and I had been sleeping together
for several months by then, the lovemaking was always
furtive and shy, our bodies only glimpsed in the flurry of

passion while before and after we were careful to keep
close enough to one another so as not to get a panoramic
view. What I found remarkable and chastening was how
relaxed everybody seemed to be. They were physical in
their nakedness without being sexual at all. They played
and cavorted as if they all had clothes on. Wading in
among them in my cutoff jeans, because I was the only
one still partially dressed, I felt as if I were the only one
exposed. It seemed that everyone but me had somehow
figured out a way to reattach the apple to the tree of
knowledge. What I wanted to do more than anything
was gawk at all the pretty girls, but gawking would have
violated the Edenic code of innocence. Instead, while
Jeff cavorted with the others as if they were his lifelong
friends, I looked casually ahead at no one in particular
at the same time that I desperately tried perfecting my
peripheral vision, ogling breasts and asses out of the cor-
ners of my eyes.

I was so distracted by the naked flesh around me
that I didn't realize that Jeff was gone. Eventually I found
him back at Hog Farm among a bunch of people doing
yoga. As I approached, a man was talking to him and the
other kids. He was older than most everybody else,

maybe in his mid-thirties, and he had short hair. I realize now he must have been a cop, one of the hundred or so brought in by the festival security team in case things at any point got out of control. In keeping with the atmosphere of benevolence and trust, the cops didn't carry guns, and aside from being older and having shorter hair, in their jeans and T-shirts they looked and acted like the rest of us. Anyway, by the time I got there, the guy was claiming to have just returned from a Zen monastery where he'd been initiated into a highly secret form of meditation, but in honor of Woodstock, he'd let us in on it. It was designed, he said, to bring Nirvana to your very bowels. More likely, though, it was the other way around, for what he proceeded to do was squat down like a sumo wrestler, and with his hands held before him palm to palm, his head bowed reverently, his eyes closed, he began to fart, fart with a capital F. I mean, these weren't just ordinary farts, these were long frank inexhaustible belches he seemed able to release at will, in different keys and registers as he moved from one position to another: now waddling like a duck with his ass cocked first to this side, then to that; now swiveling his hips like a belly dancer, swiveling and grinding them, his

arms held over his head while his head bobbed side to
side, forward and back. The Zen of farting. I have to
admit that for a while I was taken in. Only someone
with almost mystical control over his body could vigor-
ously fart at will the way he did. Then I remembered
what we'd all been eating at the free kitchen (it wasn't
called Hog Farm for nothing)—beans and brown rice.
By then everyone was flatulent enough for true enlightenment. Most people think the haze hovering over Yasgur's
farm that weekend was marijuana smoke, but me, I'm
not so sure. In any event, Jeff exclaimed "Oh wow!" and
began to imitate the man, and the others followed suit
till there were maybe fifteen or twenty new initiates all
letting it rip as they squatted and rose and waddled, lift-
ing up first this cheek, then the other, in a kind of
Animal House imitation of tai chi.

When the group broke up the cop put his arm
around one of the more "enlightened" girls. "Your spirit's just amazing," he was telling her as they went off
together.

"What a gas, no pun intended," I chuckled as Jeff
and I walked away.

"What do you mean?" There was no amusement
or irony in Jeff's face or voice.

"Jeff, you can't be serious. That guy was putting you on."

Jeff put his two hands on my shoulders. "Al," he said, looking straight into my eyes in that obsessively earnest way of his, "you gotta be more trusting, man, you're too uptight, it's like you're stuck in prison, in solitary, and there's all this beautiful shit going on outside, and you're all alone pretending there isn't 'cause you can't be part of it."

Though there was more to my skeptical detachment than mere inhibition, Jeff was right. I was uptight and too distrustful, more so than usual, to my surprise, at the very time when I should have let myself relax into what was happening around me. Among so many people, all of whom, in Joni Mitchell's words, were content to be "a cog in something turning," I had to insist on being different, better, shrewder. If, in the name of that communal embrace, they were happy to be duplicates of one another, to be heads, freaks, hippies, transparent in their openness and gullibility, I would by my very watchfulness become opaque, mysterious, dense with complexity, too streetwise and knowing to be the butt of anybody's joke. While this standoffishness prevented me from being duped, it also cheated me to some extent of the experience itself, of living it more deeply, or more richly. I was an American middle-class adolescent version of the speaker in Baudelaire's "Le Jeu," who sees the limited being of the whores and gamblers crowded around the gaming table, but at the same time recognizes in their obsessions and addictions a fiercer hold on life than he possesses, his own compulsion not to live but to stand back and observe in the nonbeing of detached superiority.

A little later, we settled down for the night on a hillside we had entirely to ourselves. Despite the night sky busy with shooting stars, the balmy weather, the one last joint we smoked, nothing could break the chill our differences had placed between us. We lay there in awkward silence, Jeff probably thinking that if Woodstock was a trial of my allegiance to the new enlightenment, then clearly I had failed it.

To give me one last chance, he asked me how much money I had, and if I'd split it with him.

"What happened to your money?" I asked. He said he'd given all of it to some Hog Farm freaks.

"And what are you gonna do with the money I give you?" Suddenly I sounded just like my father.

"Probably donate that, too," he said. "They need the bread. Anyway," he added, shrugging, "it's only money."

Only money. Only basketball. The records, the books he gave me and never wanted back. Everything abandoned with the same shrug of easy acceptance, which only now began to seem forlorn and fatalistic, not liberated in the least. Jeff hated things, I think, because things broke, things meant anxiety and worry. If you gave them away before they were taken from you, then you at least had some control, however self-destructive, over what might happen. But there was also a social dimension to this personal asceticism, for the less you had to lose, the less chance there'd be of being envied and disliked, and the easier it was to get along with others. If you had no material advantages, nothing to distinguish you from others, to set you apart from them, then nothing could be expected of you. And you had therefore nothing to live up to, which is to say, nothing to fall short of. Implicit in the communal harmony Jeff desired was an idealized family in which the collective is the happily married parents, and the individual is the child, and the love between them is unconditional, instinctive, and unlosable, falling like sunlight impartially on everyone, no matter who they are or what they do.

But for me, what I found most difficult to accept, what I instinctively resisted, was the ideal of passivity (what Jeff would have called receptivity) at the heart of this vision of the good life, the anti-perfectionist perfectionism that required its followers to abandon any upward notion of self-refinement, any notion that by dint of conscious effort, practice, dedication, you could redefine the limits of what was possible, which in art and sport defines the truly excellent. In the same way that the extraordinary care and acute awareness enacted in the form and style of the "The Geysers" contradicts or qualifies at least the psychic dissolution Gunn is celebrating, so too the musicians who encouraged us to "forget about today until tomorrow," to "let it be," to not "make plans just clap your hands," would never have become the musicians they were, would never have acquired the skills they needed to write those very songs, had they followed their own advice.

As odd as it may sound, it was my athletic training and not just my inhibition that made me balk at the counterculture's invitation to seize the day. All through grade school and high school, day in, day out, in the gym and on the playground, with single-minded dedication (or was it obsession?), I had given myself over to the discipline of learning how to play the game of basketball. I had learned to dribble, shoot, and pass with either hand. I had learned how to study my opponents and adapt my own play to their strengths and weaknesses. By subordinating myself to the discipline the game required, I'd become a better, more imaginative, more versatile player. And that convinced me I was capable of overcoming other sorts of obstacles, on and off the court. And while I eventually ran up against the limits of my physical abilities—no amount of practice would make me six foot four—that freedom to resist my limitations, to change myself, and its collateral gifts of concentration and sheer undiscourageable doggedness, would serve me later when the poems I was writing challenged my mental and imaginative powers.

Jeff had what seemed to me a horizontal vision of the good life, in which pleasure, spontaneity, and freedom were not in hock, as they were for me, to discipline and sacrifice. It may be that my more vertical understanding of the good life is partly a fancier version of the

upward mobility that drove my father's life, a transference
to the realms of art and sport of the competitive virtues
of the marketplace. Now, twenty-five years later, with
children of my own, I can admit what I would have been
too eager to deny back then: that I am, for good or ill,
my father's son, a child of the American bourgeoisie. So
too, of course, was Jeff. The new self he struggled to
become was no less dependent on the values and practices of the culture he was struggling to define himself
against. Yet when I think about the kind of life I wish for
my own children, I can't help but think my vision of the
good life, despite the many ways it unconsciously partici-
pates in the less than ideal features of American life, is
simply better than the one Jeff pursued, better because it
gives a more potentially inclusive image of human flourishing.

As we fell asleep under the stars, Jeff was no doubt
lost in his contemplation of the night sky, wholly
absorbed by the amazing light show overhead. I was
thinking that when I got back to Boston I'd have to
make up for the time away from basketball by doubling
my evening workouts.

I was awakened at dawn when someone stepping

over me accidentally kicked me in the head. The hillside
we had entirely to ourselves when we closed our eyes
was now entirely covered with people, shoulder to shoulder. They had come all through the night. Rumor was
that Route 17, the main road that led into the festival,
was backed up for miles. Ignoring the fields the organizers had reserved as parking lots, the kids grew tired of
being stuck in traffic and just abandoned their cars right
there on the road and hiked the last few miles to the
farm. Word had also gotten around that the festival
would now be open to the public, a free concert. This
decision was made less out of generosity than out of fear
that if the organizers tried to collect money from the
kids who had already crashed the gate they'd have a riot
on their hands. The festival designed to accommodate
maybe a quarter of a million people now had twice that
many. Imagine a subway car at rush hour jammed wall to
wall with people, then project that human density over a
fifty-acre farm, and you have some idea of what the
crowd was like.

By dawn on Friday the weather was already hot
and sultry, the air so humid it was like breathing someone else's spit. The humidity also seemed to bring out

the mosquitoes. I should add here that I am and always
have been a kind of human No Pest Strip. If no one else
among the five hundred thousand people at the festival
seemed bothered by the bugs, that's because all the
bugs were buzzing greedily around me, a Woodstock
Nation of them feasting at the free kitchen my body had
become.

I wasn't surprised to find that Jeff had split.
Anyway, with my eyes nearly swollen shut from the
mosquito bites I hardly cared. I spent the better part of
Friday standing in lines. I waited for several hours to use
a portable toilet only to find the stench so blindingly
repulsive that I couldn't enter. Eventually I found a relatively open field where other people were shitting and
pissing, and being by that time more desperate than shy,
I happily joined them. Then for several more hours I
waited in line at the Hog Farm free kitchen for a plate of
something that looked and tasted as if it came from someone else's stomach. It was after five by then. The concert
had begun. I was too tired and uncomfortable to work
my way into the massive audience. Besides, I had to keep
on moving to keep from getting bitten by the bugs. As
night fell, and the rains came, in a crowded field among

tents and plastic huts I lay down utterly miserable, soaking wet, and exhausted.

Just after dawn on Saturday, I saw the person I
would come to think of as the queen of Woodstock, the
living enactment of the euphoric ideal that would lead
Jeff over the years from commune to commune, drug to
drug to detox center, till he disappeared entirely from the
lives of all his old friends. I saw a naked woman in a mud
hole in the middle of a path. Kneeling in the mud, she
was slowly, almost ritualistically, taking handfuls of the
thick brown muck and smearing it down all over every
inch of her, her hair, her face, her neck, breasts, hips, and
belly, a darker caking of it on her crotch. When she had
covered herself completely, looking less like a woman
dreaming of herself as mud than like mud dreaming of
itself as woman, she began to dance among the people
swarming past her, her hips swaying, her arms held over
her head, her eyes closed, her dark smiling face all
dreamy inaccessibility. Now and again, a man or woman
would dance in front of her for a moment or two and
then pass on, while she, oblivious, continued dancing,
her trance unbreakable, the queen of Woodstock Nation
floating blissfully free beyond "the twisted reach of crazy

sorrow," beyond her name, her past, her family, even her sex, forgetting in the moment all the gravities that held her to the world beyond the moment.

Later that morning I caught a ride on a departing garbage truck. I rode on the running board, clinging to the door handle as the truck lurched precariously forward on a shoulder of the dirt road that led out to the highway, halting and inching onward against the jubilant stream of people still arriving, everybody smiling and flashing peace signs to me as I started back in the direction of my anxious father.

Come Live with Me

Auden notwithstanding, poetry is more than a mouth because a mouth is more than a mouth. Far from making nothing happen, the mouth that welcomes, insults, badgers, or implores is acting in the world, acting and provoking action in return. The mouth that vows or promises is altering the terms of life: it simultaneously performs the person it declares, the person capable of keeping faith, of being counted on, and in so doing establishes the frame of expectations in which that person's future actions will be understood and judged. As height-

ened speech in a receptive ear, poetry too can be a kind
of action. It enters the listening body to change its habits
of feeling and perception. For good or ill, it wakens the
psyche to unimagined or unrecognized or forgotten pos-
sibilities of being. It asks us to be as shrewd, tactful,
curious, or passionate as its language is, as the person
implicit in that language. Like an importunate lover,
poetry solicits our assent; it invites not a willing suspen-
sion of our disbelief but a willing submission to its own
belief that this rather than that is better, worthier, more
interesting. It woos our pliable attention to the things it
trusts, and draws it away from the things it doesn't. Each
poem pleads, whatever else its words are saying, "Come
live with me and be my love."

Perhaps that's why the young, the unattached, the
not yet hardened into who they are, seem hungriest for
poetry, why they're the ones especially vulnerable to
poetry's transformative appeal. Speaking for myself, I've
never since read with such emotional urgency as I did
in my early twenties. In those days, poetry and erotic
passion were different facets of the same desire to be
otherwise than I felt myself to be. With the same bewil-
dering helplessness, I fell for poems and poets the way I

fell for women, seeing in both the promise of a heightened life, a better life, the more remote the better.
Which may be why, as a middle-class urban Jew in the
American diaspora, I fell especially hard for Seamus
Heaney's poetry in my senior year of college. Heaney's
primordial boglands, his rural landscapes sedimented with
Christian and pre-Christian history, his ancestral embed-
dedness, couldn't have differed more profoundly from the
transient heterogeneous cityscape of my childhood and
adolescence. Heaney's Ireland, of course, wasn't the
Ireland I imagined as I read and memorized his work,
the Ireland I decided to move to when I graduated from
college. Out of my own need for a better world than the
one that raised me, a cultural and geographical cure for
what I believed to be a thin and scattershot American
existence, I partially effaced the social, religious fissures
and emotional ambivalences that everywhere pervade
and qualify the homage Heaney pays to Ireland in his
first three books. To my deracinated eye, even the sectar-
ian violence he'd begun to agonize about in poems that
appeared in magazines in the early seventies seemed glam-
orous, like the richly textured flowering of a profoundly
rooted sense of life. I responded to his poetry the same

way I responded to Irish music, which I also loved. I perceived the suffering in the song, the misery in the grace, but thought of each as part and parcel of the other. How could art convert life into so much beauty if the beauty wasn't there in the life to begin with?

In any event, just as surely as that play of Yeats's sent out in 1916 "certain men the English shot," so in 1974 Seamus Heaney's poetry sent me out to Ireland, in search of what I found or thought I found in his poems.

I sailed to Ireland from Wales, at night, across the Irish Sea, on the Holyhead/Dun Laoghaire ferry. The sky was overcast, the ocean choppy. Just the sight of water is enough to make me queasy. So how would I survive the ten-hour crossing? I asked two fellows on board if they had any Dramamine, or knew where I could get some. They assured me that a pint of Guinness would be just the ticket, just the thing I needed. "Like mither's milk," one of them said, clapping me on the shoulder. "Mither's milk," the other echoed, nodding. And off they took me to the bar. They were brothers. The older one, Jerry, was a Dublin turf accountant (the Irish term for bookie), and

the younger one, Fergus, worked in some capacity for
the civil service. They were gracious, genial, genuinely
concerned, it seemed, about my welfare. Did I know anyone in Dublin? Did I have a place to live? How long was
I staying? I said only a few months, with a college friend
who'd married an Irish woman and lived in Dublin. I
didn't mention poetry at all, my own or Heaney's, or
that I came to Ireland to live a writer's life. I didn't want
to seem pretentious or deluded. I didn't want to say
anything that might jeopardize our instantaneous
camaraderie, assuming, perhaps wrongly from past experience, that to tell a stranger "I'm a poet" would be to put
him even less at ease than if I said I was a shepherd.

After the first pint, I felt pretty good. And the
brothers were so pleased that they insisted I have another.
They rattled off a list of all the pubs in Dublin I should
go to, the ones whose bartenders pulled the Guinness
from the tap so deftly that you could etch your initials
into the creamy head and they would still be visible in
the bottom of the glass when you had finished drinking.
I said, "You know, this Guinness is amazing. I'm not sick
at all. I don't even feel the motion of the water. It's as if
we're still in port." "Are you daft, man?" Jerry exclaimed.

"We *are* in port." The massive engine rumbled. The ferry shuddered and swayed up and down, side to side, over the rough swells. I instantly turned green and wanted to die. I was too sick to feel embarrassed. Pretty soon even the brothers were wan and queasy, despite the mither's milk they went on downing. It seemed everybody was. I staggered to the men's room only to find it filled with men retching into the sinks, the toilets, even the urinals. Too desperate to wait, I went up on deck where twenty or so people were leaning close together on one side of the ferry, bent over the rails, vomiting out into the night. I wondered why they were crowding together like that when the other side of the boat was empty. And they say the Jews are clannish. I shook my head. Poor creatures of habit. Proud of my American ingenuity, I went to the other side, where nobody was, and leaned out over the Irish Sea, and what I offered to the wind the wind immediately blew back into my face and clothes. Drenched in mither's milk, I spent the rest of that long night sitting on a bench next to a woman and her small child, who vomited from time to time into a plastic bag. For hours I stared at nothing like a zombie, stupefied with nausea. I never saw Jerry or Fergus again. Next morning, when

I stepped onto Irish soil, I couldn't remember the name
of a single pub they'd recommended.

Though Carol Ann was raised on a farm in Oldtown,
forty minutes from the city, and had only lived in Dublin
with two older sisters for the past three years, nonetheless
she's become synonymous in my memory with the city
to which she introduced me. To see Dublin through her
eyes was to see a city so densely overlaid with personal
associations it was as much a psychic landscape as an
external place. It was a city of intimate spaces, of lanes,
not boulevards or avenues, of small pubs, cluttered shops,
back gardens, parlors. And with the sky perpetually overcast that autumn, with every evening and morning hazy
with the smoke of coal fires, even outside had the cozy
feel of hospitable interiority.

Even at twenty-one, Carol Ann personified domestic pleasure, familial intimacy, the reliable comforts of the
hearth. From the time she was a little girl, her parents
used to say that of all their children, five girls and a boy,
Carol Ann would be the first to marry and would raise
the largest brood. She was the heart and soul of her
tight-knit family, the mediator, the problem-solver, every-

body's confidante, the one to whom everybody turned in times of crisis, the one everybody else could lose control around because they knew she'd hold everything together. She seemed to thrive on the responsibilities of being needed. She seemed to meet the daily pressures of family life with inexhaustible patience, imagination, and grace. Nobody I'd ever met had seemed so settled, so unambivalently at home.

That's what initially attracted me to her. In the world I'd come from, to live at home or even near home after graduating from college, to visit your parents every weekend, and to live with your siblings, to socialize almost exclusively with them, would have meant dependence, immaturity, a fearful clinging to the past. In my world, you proved your individuality by the distance you put between yourself and those who raised you. Emotional as well as financial self-reliance was a sign of health. Carol Ann shared none of these American anxieties. Not that she didn't care about her independence. Rather, she believed that independence, like everything else in life, was something one attained or failed to attain within the context of family, not at the expense of family. My sort of freedom was in her eyes tantamount to exile, a desert wandering. To some extent, I must have felt the same way, yearning for the securities of home even as I spurned the only home I knew. In her I think I saw a way of breaking free from my own past, and thereby securing my individual identity, and finding at the same time in and through the very thing that proved my independence a familial refuge from the loneliness that independence brought. Too free, too unattached to any place or person, I saw in Carol Ann an exoticism of the ordinary and continuous, of a life happily circumscribed by old attachments.

And yet if she was my exotic dream of home, was I her exotic dream of freedom, her escape from the very relations who depended on her, and on whom she depended? Why else would someone so tightly stitched into the fabric of a particular community and way of life be drawn to an outsider, a foreigner, an American Jew?

Until she brought me home to meet her parents a month or so after we had started dating, it was easy not to ask these questions. Her sisters and their boyfriends had welcomed me almost instantly into their lives. The youth culture of the sixties and early seventies cut across national boundaries. Drugs, rock music, movies, and the

vaguely progressive social and political values that many
kids with a college education more or less believed in
at the time provided a kind of automatic intimacy that
could mask or minimize the underlying differences
between us. Though in the long run those differences
would seem even more profound for being small, in the
short run what we shared created, in my mind at least,
the illusion that I was one of them.

But what about the parents? Was it just naïveté
that made Carol Ann believe they would welcome and
embrace me as they had the Irish Catholic boyfriends of
her sisters? Or was I Carol Ann's unconscious or semiconscious declaration to her parents that she was not entirely
who they thought she was?

In any event, as I stood before them that Saturday
afternoon, I'd never felt more Semitic in my life.

In those days, how I acted around prospective in-
laws was the exact antithesis of how I acted around my
parents. Whereas at home I'd finickily assert anything
that distinguished my life from the life my parents led,
around the parents of my girlfriends, my strategy was to
meld, to fit in, to disappear physically, socially, philosophi-
cally, to make myself as inconspicuous as possible, not to

do anything that would call attention to myself as odd
or different, and thereby prove to them as quickly as
possible that I was just as down-to-earth, as formal, as
conservative or radical as they were, so they needn't
worry about my being with their daughter. In fact, with
Carol Ann's parents, it was all I could do not to slip into
an Irish brogue, so eager was I to let them know that,
despite whatever they assumed, I was the same as them.

"Sure now, Alan, would you like a drink?" Mr.
Rooney asked me when we were settled in the parlor for
a wee chat before tea. You bet, I answered. "What's your
pleasure?" Same as yours, sir. So there I sat, a double shot
of whisky in my trembling hand. Mr. Rooney was af-
fable enough. Mrs. Rooney, though, maintained a chilly
silence. Yes, I found Dublin lovely, not so different, after
all, from Boston. "I think Cathleen has a cousin there,
isn't that right, Cat?" Mrs. Rooney nodded. Did I know
that the previous Lord Mayor of Dublin, Robert Briscoe,
was a Jew? The Briscoes were a fine Dublin family, been
here for ages, turf accountants, all of them, isn't that right
Cat? You know that's funny, I said, I met a turf accountant on the ferry from Holyhead. "Yes," Mrs. Rooney
deadpanned. "Quite amusing."

I had a second whisky when Mr. Rooney did.
The more he drank, the more he seemed to talk into the
left breast pocket of his Harris tweed. I could make out
the occasional "ah sure" and "beJaysus," but everything
else could have been Gaelic or Linear B for all I understood. I did my best to shuck and jive, nodding, saying
Yes sir, you bet, at what I thought were the appropriate
places in his slurry sentences. By the second whisky I had
to pee, but since no one else made a move in that direction I kept silent, not wanting anyone to think I couldn't
hold my liquor. Halfway through the third drink I
couldn't wait any longer. Matter-of-factly, I asked Carol
Ann if she could tell me where the bathroom was. "The
bathroom?" Mrs. Rooney exclaimed, incredulous.
"What do you want the bathroom for?" You know,
I explained, holding up my drink, the bathroom? She
turned to Carol Ann. "Does he want to take a bath?" "I
think he means the toilet, Ma." "Oh," she said, shaking
her head as if I'd confirmed her worst suspicions, "the
loo. He wants the loo. Upstairs on the landing to the
right."

I pulled the loo door shut behind me and the
doorknob came off in my hand. As I peed I told myself

don't worry, keep cool. Then I calmly knelt by the door
and quietly tried to jimmy the lock open with my driver's license. After a good while, ten minutes or more, I
heard footsteps coming up the stairs. I held my breath.
The footsteps paused outside the door. Then they turned
around and left. Furiously, I continued working, sweat-
ing and cursing, my driver's license jammed in a lock that
wouldn't budge. I could hear my mother saying, "If
you'd only gone to Israel like your father and I wanted,
none of this would have happened." A little later the footsteps returned. I heard Rosemary, Carol Ann's younger
sister, giggling, whispering to someone, "I think Alan's
locked inside the loo." "Yes I am," I whispered back.
"Could you please let me out of here?" My when-in-
Rome philosophy now in utter shambles, I returned to
the parlor where the girls were laughing. Even Mrs.
Rooney seemed to smile. Oblivious, Mr. Rooney
muttered, "Sure now Alan, as I was saying. . . ."

After tea, Carol Ann took me for a walk around
the farm. As we wandered through the fields and clam-
bered over hedges, for the first time we talked about the
future, a subject we'd studiously avoided, not wanting to
wrinkle in any way the pleasure of our growing intimacy.

She wanted to know if I felt at home in Ireland, could I imagine living here. I said I did feel at home in Ireland, with her siblings at least, if not her parents, though she assured me that her mother would eventually come around. I wasn't so sure, but at the time it didn't matter. I was happy and couldn't imagine feeling otherwise.

Carol Ann knew that I'd applied for a Stegner fellowship at Stanford University. I'd applied for one the year before, and since that application had been rejected, I assumed this year's application would be rejected too. If the Stegner did not come through, as it most likely wouldn't, then I would definitely stay in Ireland.

Though I spent most evenings now at Carol Ann's apartment, I was still nominally living with my college friend and fellow poet, Jason, and his wife, Bernardine. Until I met Carol Ann, Jason and I had been living in a poetry dream world. We'd read and write all day, then pub-crawl in the evenings in search of Dublin's literary world. In those first few months, we met a host of writers—the poet Brendan Kennelly, who taught at Trinity; Peter Fallon, the founder of Gallery Press; and many others whose names I can't recall. But not Heaney. Though Heaney lived in Wicklow at the time and often came

into the city, for one reason or another our paths just
never crossed. The poets we did meet were welcoming,
and very generous with praise for the American poets we
would mention—Frost, Roethke, Williams, Lowell,
Wright, and others—but remarkably ungenerous toward
each other, especially Heaney, much to my surprise. This
was just around the time that *North* was published, the
book that made Heaney really famous overseas. In England it sold over six thousand copies in its first month
alone. It did almost as well in America. That fall and win-
ter, it seemed, Heaney's name was everywhere. It's
understandable that his fellow Irish poets would feel a
touch of envy. "Ah, sure, fame is wonderful," one poet
told me, "except when other poets get it." But there was
more than envy in their criticism, which wasn't directed
at the work itself so much as at the readers of the work,
those like me who were uncritically enthusiastic about it.
On more than one occasion I heard someone say that
Heaney wasn't sentimental, but that his readers often
were, especially in America, where everyone's nostalgic
for some lost world or other. I was taken aback at first,
though eventually I came to see how just the criticism
was, at least of me. But beyond that, once I got used to

the severity, I came to imagine in the lack of generosity
these poets seemed to show each other a form of heightened respect, proceeding from profound engagement.
For each other's work, if not always for their own, their
shit-detectors, like the eyes of Cerebus, never rested.
And while this skepticism, this refusal to be had,
appeared to make them less susceptible to the literary passions I was prone to, it may also have expressed a deeper
urgency toward poetry and its effect on life that in the
long run may have been more serious, if not exactly
more intense.

   After the pubs closed, Jason and I would stay up
late into the night, talking, singing, reading poetry to
one another before the coal fire in the sitting room. Bernardine taught grade school and was usually asleep by the
time we got home and gone by the time we'd awakened,
so aside from weekends we hardly ever saw her. Our
friendship was intense and all-encompassing, an extension of a shared commitment to the art we loved.
Bernardine seemed initially to accept the regimen we
had established for ourselves. She accommodated me,
our friendship, our mutual obsession; she took it as a
matter of course, because her husband was a poet, that

this was the sort of life a poet led. Had I not been lonely
for the company of women, I'd have been completely
happy. And once I met Carol Ann I was, or thought I was.

Even then I knew that Carol Ann did not entirely
share my enthusiasm for poetry. For her it had the status
of a hobby, an honorable but peripheral activity you did
on weekends or holidays while the rest of life was taken
up with the essentials, the real work, of providing for
and being with your family. That you'd arrange a life
primarily around an art, that you'd sacrifice domestic
pleasures for the sake of poetry, as I in my fanatical devotion was prepared to do, was wholly alien to her way of
thinking. Though she didn't say so, she had no desire to
be the self-sacrificing midwife to my muse.

Yet in the early stages of our relationship, and
especially that afternoon, she pretended to be more toler-
ant of poetry than she was, if not more interested in it,
just as I pretended to be more willing and even eager to
take on the responsibilities of family life. She said she'd
accommodate as best she could my ambitions and enthu-
siasms. And I said I could easily devote myself to the
perfections of the life as well as the perfections of the
work. Without realizing it, we were leading each other

to expect a person neither of us would be capable of being. I read into what she told me what I desired to hear: that she would respect my aspirations the way Bernardine apparently respected Jason's. Carol Ann likewise heard in my assurances that once the two of us had settled down, poetry would shrink into the margins of an otherwise conventional domestic life.

We were walking now along a road that ran between two fields, tall hedges on either side of us. "Come on," she said, taking my hand, "there's something I want to show you." At the intersection up ahead was a small knoll with a low stone wall around it. We entered through a metal gate. It was her family graveyard. Gravestones of generations of Rooneys lay higgledy-piggledy across the grass, the older ones tilted this way or that, so worn away and weathered that the lettering had mostly disappeared into the stone, and what remained was like a partially recorded telegraph:

> Her   ies   ean (1867–1 03)
> bel ved son
> o   ary an   eamus
>
> Maure n daughte
> of P t an   Marg   et
> Lies wit   hrist ou   Lor

The newer ones were upright, shiny, the names, the dates, the Lord Have Mercys chiseled cleanly enough, it seemed, to last forever. Carol Ann pointed to the smooth grass in the far corner. "That's where my mother and father will go," she said. Then, as an afterthought, "And the rest of us."

Even by 1974, my family was scattered across the globe: my brother and his wife in New York, my sister in Michigan, I now on the other side of the Atlantic. Only my parents remained in Boston, and even they talked of eventually moving to Florida or California. It never occurred to me to wonder or care about where I'd be buried. For Carol Ann, though, the idea of where her body would be laid to rest was what made even the possibility of living outside Ireland so intolerable. When I would daydream aloud about residing even for a few years in this or that city or country, she'd never say, I couldn't bear the thought of living there, but rather, I couldn't bear the thought of being buried there. It was as if on some deep level she believed that death would not be something to be feared if you were buried with your family in the same place where you were born and lived; that death would mean extinction only in a strange land where you had no past.

A few days later, I wrote a poem about this incident, the first poem I ever wrote for Carol Ann. I no
longer have a copy of it, but I remember that it ended
with my imagining her funeral, years after her last
thought of me, her Irish husband and Irish children weeping as her coffin is lowered into the ground. I wanted to
express the painful sense of cultural difference that the
moment seemed to dramatize; that, and the jealousy I
felt for a future I suddenly grew afraid I wouldn't share.
Carol Ann disliked the poem. The day had been so
lovely, she said, and then I had to go and turn it into
something troubling and melancholy. She was right, of
course. But that wouldn't be the last time she'd feel
injured by my penchant for finding sadness and complexity in moments she believed were purely joyful. Though
I shouldn't have been, I was surprised and disappointed
by her reaction. I tried explaining that the fears expressed
about the future weren't meant to diminish the pleasure
of the moment so much as to make that pleasure more
intense and valuable, the way Hardy does in "During
Wind and Rain." Well, she'd never read the Hardy
poem. And anyway this was her experience, not Hardy's,
and I had ruined it for her.

Even then, so early in our life together, she associated poetry, my poetry, with betrayal—not just because of all the time I spent writing, but because the things I wrote so often contradicted her sense of our relationship. Poetry eventually became for both of us a sharp reminder that there were distances between us, distances that came to seem more painful the more intimate we grew.

A few months later, in the early spring, Carol Ann's uncle, Thomas Rooney, died after a long illness. She wanted me to come with her to the funeral. What with my melancholy temperament, she wryly offered, it ought to suit me.

To my surprise, the funeral mass was not remarkably different from the Jewish memorial services I remembered from my childhood, especially in terms of length, solemnity, and my own restlessness. And if you substituted Latin prayers for Hebrew prayers, priest for rabbi, Christ for Adonai, the burial too was oddly similar. What I found profoundly different, though, was what happened in between. The funeral procession stopped twenty yards or so from the gate to the Rooney graveyard. Mr. Rooney, his two surviving brothers, and his son, Pat, lifted the coffin from the hearse and then walked with it on their shoulders three times around the small knoll before entering. Later, no one could tell me what the custom meant. Did they circle three times for the Trinity? Or did the gesture signify something older, a vestige of some pre-Christian Celtic ritual, or an amalgam of the two? Nobody knew. Carol Ann could only say that that was how they buried people here. I thought of the line from Heaney's "Bogland," "Every layer they strip / Seems camped on before," and also of his more recent poem, "Funeral Rites," from *North*—the way the pagan past and Christian present are superimposed on each other as Heaney turns his contemporary mourners into Norsemen driving away from the imagined funeral, not past Strangford and Carlingford but "past Strang and Carling Fjords / the cud of memory / allayed for once, arbitration of the feud placated. . . ."

That the custom had an unknown origin only enhanced, it seemed, the comfort it bestowed. By participating in a ceremony reaching back beyond their personal lives, even beyond their collective memory, all the members of the community seemed able to connect their perishable selves to an imperishable corporate life. They grieved for Thomas Rooney, but in the ancient cus-

Is this what poetry — its measured language, its monuments of images — does?

tomary rhythms of that grief there was a compensating
solace, a sense of life, true life, life at its most essential, as
something larger and more durable than any individual. I
began to understand a little better Carol Ann's attachment to her home, and at the same time her impatience
with my own morbidity, my death obsession. Death was
fearful for her, as it was for me, but it wasn't an obsessive
fear, a constant terror, because for her the individual, the
solitary self, was hardly all there was. With no stable and
extended communal world as part of my identity, I felt
that nothing of me (but my poems maybe) would survive
my life, that the world would die when I died, and that
life itself bereft of such communal underpinnings was as
perilous and insubstantial as the membrane of a bubble
stretched over the abyss.

Sometimes Carol Ann would jokingly dismiss my
mortal terrors; other times, though, they'd anger her. It
wasn't only that she found the narcissism tedious, but
also, I think now, that she read within that narcissism a
congenital incapacity for the unqualified allegiances that
held her world together.

By April, I had lined up for myself a part-time teaching
job for the fall semester at a local college. By then, too,

I'd moved in with Carol Ann. We were even talking about marriage, which her parents stoically accepted, provided I agree to raise our children in the Catholic faith. Her father said that as a wedding gift he'd give us a hundred acres of the farm and farm it for us, which ought to bring in money enough for us to live on. I was both enchanted at the prospect and uneasy—now that it seemed possible—about settling outside the States. Then the word from Stanford came that I had landed the Stegner.

Carol Ann did her best to celebrate with me. She took me out to dinner, and we drank several toasts to my good fortune. By the time we got home, though, she'd had too much to drink to hide her feelings. She was devastated. Once I was back in America, Ireland, herself, the life we planned together, would be a distant dream. That opportunity, she said, would lead to others, and since my only true commitment was to poetry, not to her, I'd go wherever that commitment led. Don't be silly, I tried assuring her. It's just a year, and she should come with me. It would be a great adventure for both of us. A premarital honeymoon. Carol Ann was not persuaded. That night she lay beside me weeping inconsolably, as if she saw too clearly, even then, the heartache that the future held in store.

She did join me in California a few months after I got settled. But since she was only able to obtain a three-month, nonrenewable fiancée visa, when it expired we would have to either tie the knot or say goodbye. To Carol Ann, we chose the lesser of two evils. Her parents thought that she was living with a college friend of hers who'd settled in the area. She was certain that if they found out we were living together, much less that we were getting married outside the Church, they'd have her excommunicated. She hated the secrecy of it all. She was terrified that somehow her parents would discover what we were doing. To pacify her, to make the wedding not a wedding, and therefore not a sin, I bought two plastic puzzle rings, not gold rings, for the civil ceremony at the San Jose County courthouse. In keeping with the farce, on the drive over to San Jose, Carol Ann was fiddling with the rings so nervously they came unraveled. She hardly noticed and went on twisting them like rosary beads between her fingers. At the courthouse, we desperately tried to put them back together as we stood in line with other couples. We said "I do" before the bored, impatient judge with the raggedy chain links of the two rings dangling from our fingers.

Later that day, as soon as we got back to our apartment, Carol Ann locked herself inside the bedroom and wept for hours. I stood outside the door, telling her that things would be okay, that her parents would never find out about this, that we'd have a proper Catholic wedding when we returned to Ireland, as we surely would. The more I spoke, the more I came to doubt the truth of what I said, and yet I went on saying it, saying anything to make her feel less scared, less lonely, and, if truth be told, to feel myself less guilty. Would there ever come a time when our desires, our dreams, our profoundest hopes, wouldn't stand so starkly opposed, when happiness for one wouldn't mean unhappiness for the other, when my good luck wouldn't mean her bad? I remembered with a shudder how only six months earlier I lay beside her on the night I heard from Stanford, saying many of the same things I was saying now. As if it were an emblem of my divided loyalties, of Carol Ann's as well, an emblem of what our marriage was and always would be, I saw us lying together in her Dublin flat, both of us sad because I would be leaving, but I now also half-ashamed because I wasn't only sad; even as I tried to solace her and needed solacing myself, with my arm around her, my one hand moving tenderly across her back, her shoulders, I had to hold in check the impulse to lift my other hand in a triumphant fist and shake it as she went on crying.

FANATICS

When Billy "the Kid" Lazarus called me to announce
that he'd converted to Hasidic Judaism, I thought, okay,
so Billy the Kid is now Billy the Yid. What else is new?

I wanted to see this fresh turn his life had taken as
no different from the others: like his sudden craze for
weightlifting in high school, for cars in college; like his
brief stint as a Jew for Jesus the previous summer when
he visited me and my first wife, Carol Ann, in Ireland.
So what if Saul, after an interlude of being Paul, was Saul
again, but in a purer way. Yet as I listened to him happily

describe his life as a Lubavitcher—the long hours of
study, the arduous yet joyous dedication it required, the
heady sense of chosenness, the mystical connection to
the Torah, to the Jews he lived among, to God himself,
his voice now inflected with the Yiddish intonations of
our elders—I wondered if all his other passions weren't
just so many dress rehearsals for this last big fling. Anyway, this was 1978, just after the mass suicide in Guyana
of the followers of Jim Jones, whose cult, the People's
Temple, had originated in San Francisco, just miles from
where I was living at the time. Even more so than the
rest of the country, the Bay area was all abuzz with cults
and sects and the evils of fanatical devotion. There was
nothing evangelical to Billy's faith in Jesus as his personal savior. He never tried to proselytize. He was quite
happy to be the only one among his friends who wasn't
damned. But Yahweh was a jealous God. And now, as a
Lubavitcher Hasid, a member of the evangelical wing of
Jewish Orthodoxy, wasn't Billy, or Shlomo as he now
called himself, obligated to bring all Jews back into the
fold? Wouldn't he be especially solicitous of me, his oldest friend?

My worst suspicions were confirmed when, just

before hanging up, he mentioned that he'd be spending Hanukkah with a fellow Lubavitcher whose parents lived in Oakland. He planned to visit me (just me, not me and Carol Ann) shortly after he arrived. And he prayed to *Ha Shem,* blessed be his name, that I would listen with an open mind to what he had to tell me.

Only after we hung up did I realize that Billy had done all the talking. Almost a year since we had seen each other, yet he never once asked me how I was doing, what was new, how Carol Ann was. He'd always been extremely interested in my career. Though he himself had no artistic inclinations (in college he was pre-med), he'd always taken a kind of sentimental pleasure in my poetry, proud in an almost fatherly way that someone so close to him could do and succeed at what seemed so foreign to his interests. In the years I'd been at Stanford, first as a fellow in the writing program, then as a lecturer, he'd always made a point of asking me what I was working on, or if anything I'd written had appeared in magazines he might have heard of. He liked to brag about me to our old friends. But God apparently (being the jealous God he is) had claimed whatever interest Billy used to take in this side of my life. My wounded vanity aside, what troubled me most about our conversation was the sheer relief, the stainless-steel serenity his voice possessed. How free his speech now seemed of that congenital yet touching urgency that used to make his words stumble and trip over one another in their hurry to get said, the sense anxiously running ahead of the sentences, which often spilled out in a pell-mell rush of fractured syntax, malaprops, and comically mixed metaphors. He once told me that he hated to be in a car that someone else was driving because he didn't like to put his life in someone else's foot's hand. He used to say things like "mea capo" for "mea culpa," "negligee" for "negligent" ("Hey, so, you know, so I was a little negligee, so sue me"), and he once bemoaned how he had squandered away his four years at college, adding, "For all *intensive* purposes I have no education." This new voice was clear, unstrained, and eloquently simple. The sentences flowed from his tongue so gracefully they almost seemed to speak themselves.

The more I brooded on how different he sounded, the more I could see Billy as he used to be, not just in college and high school, but in grade school as well, and even earlier. I could see him in that third-floor apartment where he was raised—the small flat made even smaller, more claustrophobic, by his two stepsisters, on whom his parents doted; his obese, often out-of-work musician stepfather; and his mother, who looked like a human thimble in her faded housedress, diminutive and dumpy, compensating for her small size with titanic fury as she cooked and cleaned. Billy's biological father died in the Korean War. Since my father had been a mess sergeant during World War II and never killed anything but cows, I admired Billy for having a dead war hero for a dad. Even though he'd never known him, Billy talked about his father all the time. He even carried around a crumpled photograph of him in uniform. Unlike his stepfather, who mostly sat around the house all day picking on Billy, his "real" dad (that's how Billy would refer to him) had been brave, hardworking, handsome, fun to be around, "a regular prince," he used to say, mimicking his mother. Billy's obsession with his "real" dad (not to mention that most of what the family lived on came directly from his "real" dad's army pension) must have fueled his stepfather's low-grade continuous hostility. In any event, he couldn't see Billy without complaining: Why can't you clean your room the way your sisters do? Why do you have to be so noisy? What are you, made of wood? Do I have to tell you everything a thousand times? Invariably, Billy would talk back, and the fight would escalate, his mother cleaning furiously all around her son and husband while they went on shouting at each other until her son was finally shut up in his room.

If you can call it a room. Just off the kitchen, windowless, no bigger than a jail cell, it had probably been a pantry once. One wall of it was brick. The room held nothing but a bed, a tiny dresser, and the baseball bat that Billy kept under the bed. More a pressure cooker than a room, in which for eighteen years Billy seemed to boil up more than grow up, jittery, high-strung, breathless with angers and appetites that the small apartment and his room especially seemed to intensify by cramping. There he would steam and simmer for hours at a time, until he'd finally get the bat out and beat the brick wall with it, his explosive anger reflected in the thousands of tiny brick shards that were always peppering his sheets.

By the time he left home, his appetites and desires lived in his body the way his body had lived in the room. It was as if whatever limits, forms, proprieties, or expectations he encountered became another incarnation of the room itself, each impulse another bat to beat the brick wall with.

It saddens me to think that the very qualities I loved in Billy might have been the ones that most tormented him. His wild impulsiveness, his ever-restless hunting after more and better, the edgy speed with which he gobbled up each pleasure as if some unseen hand were poised to snatch it from him if he didn't eat it quick—the very things that made him, in my eyes, fun and sometimes dangerous to be around—were, I see now, the residue of thwarted need, ancient trauma.

Of course, even back in college I knew that Billy was a problem to himself. But in those days, who wasn't? Seeing him through the lens of my timidity and inhibition, I envied his honesty, his courageous refusal to abide by codes of behavior I disparaged in superficial ways but with which I was enthralled in all the ways that mattered. As someone often paralyzed with self-consciousness and doubt, I found Billy's impetuosity exhilarating. If most of us, in theory anyway, were anarchists, abstract celebrants of openness and spontaneity, enemies of constraint and inhibition, Billy seemed to be the thing itself. And I admired him for it.

I remember early in my freshman year taking Billy to an open-mike poetry reading in the student center. I at the time was too shy to read, but I was curious about the poetry the other campus poets wrote. Billy, the pre-med major, had no interest in anybody's poetry but mine. His overheated nervous system, however, ill-equipped him for the concentration and discipline pre-med demanded. In fact, the grind itself aroused in him from the start the impulse to rebel, which was probably why he chose that onerous course of study in the first place. He was always on the verge of flunking out. That he managed not to, given how little he studied, was a measure of his natural ability. In any event, the more he fell behind in his studies, the more vulnerable he was to anything, even a poetry reading, that might distract him from the work he was supposed to be doing.

There were twenty or so kids in the room, a few genuinely attentive, but most just pretending to be, lending an ear to other people's poetry so other people in turn would lend an ear to them (with interest) when they got up to read. Each reader sat in a chair at the front of the room. The first poet gave a rather long introduction to his poem, saying, "I was walking back to my

dorm from the library the other day and saw the sun setting, dropping down behind the treetops, and I realized
now that I'm older and busier that I never stop to watch
the sunset anymore, I never just let go and groove on the
moment like I used to when I was younger, so I went
back to my room and wrote this poem." Then he started
reading: "I was walking back to my dorm from the
library the other day and saw the sun setting, dropping
down behind the treetops, and I realized. . . ." I remember another kid reading a sort of Ashberian montage, full
of abrupt shifts in tone and diction, ironic undercuttings
and deflations. The end went something like this: "The
almost misting of your violent nuance now at last drains
you from the source they told me you could never find.
So it is all weather, news, laughter, a dog barks, someone
is eating yogurt, I wish I were dead, or fucking, I guess."
Billy sat beside me like an engine whose idle had been
set too high, with one knee trembling, one finger fiddling with his moustache, his big jaw twitching.

    The last reader was a cross between Rilke and Jug-
head. His black beret, black shirt, and black trousers
made his complexion seem paler and more ravaged than
it was. I don't remember much about his poem except

that it was long and hard to follow, an interminable smear of sensibility in which vagueness masqueraded as profundity. I thought it was terrific. I was so entranced by the way the poet swayed and chanted that I didn't notice till the poem was nearly over that Billy had crossed the room and was now standing right in front of the poet, looking down at him as he intoned the final lines: "I, too, have known the joys of rum. I have walked down what other men call sidewalks." The room was hushed. The bard looked up at Billy. Billy, smiling, stuck one finger up into the bard's nose and nearly lifted him off his chair by the nostril. "Well, asshole," he said before he let him go, "I pick what other men call noses."

As we hurried from the room, all I could say was "Jesus!" Billy just shrugged. He seemed as startled as I was by what he'd done. That's how he always was after doing something outrageous, like a sobering drunk only dimly aware of what he might or might not have said the night before. He felt bad about embarrassing the poet. I said something encouraging like "Don't worry, Billy. By the turn of the century no one'll remember this ever happened." Then, because he really did feel bad, I added, "Anyway, I guess it was a shitty poem, after all." He shook his head sadly. "Yeah, I know, but it wasn't just the poem, Al." But whatever else it was that made him do what he did he couldn't say.

Just as he couldn't say a few months later why he hurled the baseball through the plate glass window of the dining hall. We were playing catch in the quadrangle. It must have been around exam time, for in my memory the quadrangle was entirely deserted, everyone else holed up cramming in their rooms or at the library, only me and Billy throwing the ball back and forth, each of us chanting "Hum baby lotta fire, lotta fire" as the other threw. The dining hall, too, was empty. Only the tables and chairs nearest the massive window were visible within the gloom. After a half hour or so, I said I'd had enough, threw the ball to Billy, and started back to the dorm. Billy was standing before the plate glass. He was flipping the ball in his hand, up and down, up and down, staring at his reflection as if admiring himself. I heard the shattering boom. The window was a panicky spiderweb of cracks around the jagged black hole where Billy's face had been. Billy just stood there, peering with a look of puzzlement into the shadowy room beyond the glass, at whatever it was his reflected face had been obscuring.

"What are you crazy or something? You wanna get suspended?" But he just kept on staring, oddly calm, at ease, as if a spring that had been tightening inside him had suddenly been sprung, though I could sense that it was already tightening again as I anxiously rehearsed the story we would tell, that it was all just an accident, that we were playing catch, that the ball just got away from us, and . . . "Al," he interrupted, "no problem. I'll handle it." Then he walked back toward the dorm, saying we probably ought to hit the books.

Billy looked pretty much as I expected him to look: fedora hat, full beard, black suit, white shirt unbuttoned at the collar. If I was somewhat ready, though, for his appearance, I was wholly unprepared for how he greeted Carol Ann. It had been only a year since he had spent two months working on her father's farm in Ireland. During his stay there, he and Carol Ann became good friends. With her long brown hair, pale skin, green eyes, and slender figure made more shapely by the tight-fitting clothes she liked to wear, Carol Ann was every Jewish mother's nightmare. Billy was drawn to women, any woman, with a kind of animal urgency he was unable to disguise. Some were repelled by this, but some found it irresistible, enough anyway so that he always had a girl-friend. But the girlfriend he had on any given day never turned out to be the one he wanted. It almost seemed he was compelled to sleep with any and every woman who attracted him in order not to think about her anymore. In any event, whenever a pretty woman passed him in the street, especially the ones with other men, he'd stop dead in his tracks and gawk with such frank longing you'd think that she was paradise itself, and that without her he would hate his life. Carol Ann was charmed by his gruff directness. And he in turn was charmed by her gentle mockery of it. Their devotion to me made it safe for them to flirt and banter. And by the end of the sum-mer they were pals. Or so Carol Ann thought.

    Billy turned away as she came up to embrace him. He wouldn't look directly at her. She asked how his family was. Fine, he said—to me, as if *I* had asked the question. She asked him if he had seen a mutual friend of ours, and he said no, again to me, not her. Would he like something to eat or drink? No thanks, he replied, looking again in my direction as if an invisible harness strapped around his head was pulling it away from Carol

Ann whenever she would speak. After a few minutes of this, visibly hurt and angry, she left the room. I asked him, What's up? How could you treat Carol Ann like that?

He ignored the question. Or rather he answered it by saying that the fate of the Jewish community as a whole, and beyond the Jewish community, of mankind itself, is tied to the particular fate of every individual Jew, believers and unbelievers alike. He talked about the 613 *mitzvot* (commandments), which govern every aspect, every moment, of a Hasid's life, and how a life lived according to the Law infuses everything—lovemaking, eating, even bodily functions—with holiness and joy. Billy *davened* as he talked, his upper body swaying back and forth as if in prayer, the way the old Jews used to in the synagogue I went to as a child. The more I watched him, the more it seemed that the holy joy he felt (and I had no doubt that he felt it) was not a personal joy but the joy of personal extinction, the joy of the body trans-formed through ritual and unremitting discipline into a transpersonal vessel for the holy spirit, the living God. Wasn't that the purpose of the black suit, the earlocks, the beard, the *tefillin* the Hasid straps to the hand and

forehead every weekday morning? Not just a way of
saying that the self is this, not that; is Jew, not gentile;
Hasid, not mere Jew; Lubavitcher Hasid, not mere
Hasid. But also a way of saying that the self has no identity except that corporate one. Not just a way of saying
this transcendent unity has been achieved, but also a
reminder that only with great and constant vigilance is
it sustained, is it preserved. Implicit in the uniformity
of dress and the ritual circumspection of every single
moment of the day is the recognition of anarchic appe-
tite, unexpungeable violence, unbridled selfishness and
egotism that require an equally violent or comprehensive
set of rituals to be kept in line. Yahweh wouldn't be such
a jealous God if his children weren't so easily distracted.
If we weren't so forgetful of his word, he wouldn't need
to repeat himself so often, constantly reminding us to
love "the Lord your God with all your heart, and with
all your soul, and with all your might."

It was no surprise that Billy seemed most like his
old self when he described the terrible and never-ending
struggle he endured to purify himself, to square his
earthly nature with the heavenly rule of law. Sexual ab-
stinence was especially difficult, he said. Since his

conversion eight months earlier, he'd hardly so much as
looked at a woman. In the Hasidic culture, unmarried
men and women are carefully segregated, and what contact they do have is carefully monitored. Unlawful
sexuality, including even sexual thoughts or impulses of
any kind, is so proscribed that the Hasid guards against it
even while he sleeps or prays. For instance, during prayers he wears a *gartel,* or belt, the purpose of which is to
cordon off the upper, more spiritual part of the body
from the lower, more earthly part, so that no profane
thoughts might interrupt, contaminate his heavenly communion. Some yeshiva students (and Billy was one of
them) sew shut the pockets to their pants so there's
less temptation to masturbate while studying. It was also
moving to hear Billy describe how embarrassing he
found the jeering and taunts his dress and appearance usually elicited from people on the street. That he felt any
mortification whatsoever only proved, he said, how
entangled he still was in the snares of the ego, how far he
had to go to reach the serene detachment and selfless
devotion that genuine piety required.

   If Billy was intent on extinguishing the ego, I, in
my life and work, at least from his point of view, was rev-

eling in it. For Billy, there was no such thing as a career or the personal gratifications and excitements that a career entails. There was devotion to God, and the God-given Law by which that devotion is achieved. The rest of life had value only insofar as it enabled or didn't interfere with that devotion. I was equally single-minded in my devotion to the art of poetry, and to establishing a life that would enable me to do the work I felt compelled to do. But to think that there was anything worth writing or reading that didn't glorify the Creator or the life that he demanded we, as Jews, should live, was to Billy's way of thinking at best deluded *chutzpah,* at worst unimaginable blasphemy.

I listened as Billy calmly, righteously, went on hammering away at everything on which my life was built. I wasn't angry or offended. Armed with my own unassailable pieties, I listened with superior, somewhat contemptuous amusement. For I too (though I didn't recognize this then) was a true believer, and the faith I clung to with no less fervor not only had its sacred doctrine, replete with clear and definitive prescriptions and proscriptions; it also had its spiritual leader. Billy's was Menachem Mendel Schneerson, the rebbe of the

Lubavitcher movement; mine was Yvor Winters, the
late rebbe of the Stanford Creative Writing Program.

Winters had died in 1968, six years before I came
to Stanford. But he was still very much a living presence
to me and the other students in the writing program. As
aspiring writers who had yet to publish (not for lack of
trying), we identified with his outsider status in the literary world. Early in his career, Winters had abandoned
many of the modernist techniques and assumptions that
had governed the work of his contemporaries, and that
still governed to some extent much of the work of mine.
His poetry and criticism (*In Defense of Reason* especially)
were our sacred texts, our Torah and Talmud. Just as
Billy believed that the Torah was not only the law of the
Jewish people, but the cosmic law of the universe itself,
so we believed that Winters's definitions and prescriptions were true not only for the poetry he wrote and
admired, but for any poetry at all that aspired to be death-
less and universal. By dividing all poets since the
eighteenth century into sheep and goats, into those
enlightened few whose procedures were essentially
rational and metrical, and the unenlightened essentially
romantic many for whom poetry was emotional release,

immersion in irrational nature, Winters gave us, ignorant
as we all were then, and insecure about our ignorance, a
heady sense of mastery over everything we didn't know.
We read the poets Winters recommended and ignored
the ones he claimed provided only a dangerously incomplete account of what it means to be alive—dangerous
because if you took the ideas seriously, if you put them
to the test of experience, then you would either change
your way of thinking and writing, as Winters had, or,
like Hart Crane, Sylvia Plath, and John Berryman, you'd
go mad and kill yourself. That most poets of the irrational did not go mad or kill themselves only proved that
they had isolated the poetry they wrote from the lives
they led, trivializing both in the process. Like Crane,
Plath, and Berryman, we too had the courage of our convictions, but our convictions were life-enhancing, not
life-threatening. For us, the act of writing and reading
had all the urgency of a morality play in which the self
heroically confronts the brute facts of irrational nature
and, in the confrontation, renews, strengthens, and
extends the fragile boundary of human consciousness.

This is not to say we lived exemplary lives. Far
from it. In the bars, in the streets, in each other's bed-

rooms, we caroused and rioted, while on the page we
moralized about the dangers of excess. We lived like
Rimbaud even while we wrote like Jonson. In fact, I
sometimes wonder now if the almost magical power we
ascribed to metrical control didn't in some way license
and legitimize, not restrain, the chaos of the life we
led. So long as our poems scanned, so long as we made
rationally defensible statements, in meter, about what
happened to us, so long as we believed that we had
understood and mastered our experience, we were free
to do whatever the hell we wanted.

I don't mean to condescend to who I was back
then. Like new converts to any faith, I was more Wintersian than Winters himself, certainly more Wintersian
than my teachers, Donald Davie and Kenneth Fields. But
even that simplified Wintersianism was incredibly valuable. Through his anthology, *Quest for Reality,* which I
read constantly, I was introduced to many wonderful
poets I otherwise might not have read, poets like Fulke
Greville, Frederick Goddard Tuckerman, Mina Loy, Elizabeth Daryush, Janet Lewis, and Edgar Bowers. Because
I learned from Winters that great poems are written "one
by one / And spaced by many years, each line an act /

Through which few labor, which no men retract," I gave
myself the freedom not to worry overmuch if this or that
poem I was writing was even very good; even the bad
poems were necessary preparation for the good ones up
ahead, the good ones necessary for the great ones. As a
result, I learned how to be patient and persistent, to go at
my own pace. If my Wintersianism helped inflate my
long-term expectations for what I might achieve, at one
and the same time it helped deflate my short-term expectations so I could go on learning as I wrote. Even the
more juvenile expressions of that enthusiasm were exhilarating and necessary. The circular logic that came with
believing I was writing against the spirit of the age gave
me what all young poets need, the stubborn arrogance to
go on writing no matter how discouraging my prospects
were, no matter how much the world (literary or otherwise) was telling me it had no need for or interest in
anything I wrote. Wasn't I in this respect like Billy too?
For in the same way that persecution and suffering are
for the Hasid a sign of divine election, of God's interest
in his chosen few, so that the more he suffers, the more
assured he is of his salvation, so I believed the health of
poetry depended on the metrical poems I and my fellow

students were writing in defiance of the barbarian, non-
metrical hordes. The very fact that we had trouble
publishing our poems only confirmed their value. The
more the literary world neglected us, the more convinced we were that only through our poems could
the literary world be saved.

That afternoon I couldn't have acknowledged,
much less have seen, any of these similarities between me
and Billy. My allegiance, after all, was to rational control,
intellectual judgment, moderation of feeling—qualities
you couldn't have too much of, could you? Hasidism, on
the other hand, was the Jewish Orthodox equivalent of
romantic excess. Moreover, didn't Hasidism and Romanticism both arise at roughly the same time, in the mid-
to-late eighteenth century? And like Romanticism in the
arts, didn't the Hasidic movement favor energy over
order, enthusiasm over learning, mystical release over
rational control? Wasn't Hasidism pantheistic in its root
assumption, that God was everywhere, in everything?
And didn't the Hasid strive for dissolution into what Gershom Scholem calls "the everlasting unity"? Never mind
that this is a highly distorted and reductive picture of
both Hasidic mysticism and Romantic art, created by a

highly distorted and reductive understanding of Yvor
Winters. What this picture enabled me to do was sit back
and listen to Billy in a luxuriously condescending mood
of pity.

Poor Billy, I thought, with his black suit, his
arcane ritual observances, his dietary restrictions, his 613
laws, his new Old World voice—what did all this mean
but that he now had turned upon himself, his body, his
very being, the restless fury he once directed at his bedroom wall and, later on, at the conventions by which
people tried to make him live. Wasn't he, at every
moment of every day, hammering away at any impulse,
desire, look, or thought that didn't fit the impersonal
mold of perfect piety? So what if he seemed happier,
calmer, less edgy than I'd ever known him. He paid too
steep a price for that serenity. All he'd done, I remember
thinking, was exchange a universe of accident, surprise,
doubt, and adventure for one in which nothing happens,
no common cold, no massacre, no rape, no child abuse,
not the slightest blink of an eye, that isn't tied directly to
the Lord our God, Ruler of the Universe, blessed be his
name. Billy had escaped the bad dream of his independence and autonomy into the womb of *Yiddishkeit,* and

what I imagined he had found there was what his family never gave: absolute unbreakable connection to the lives of others, a sense, too, that as a member of the tribe he had an absolute importance, that the very structure of the moral world depended on him and his devotions, his every action as a Jew. Thus, the very thing that extinguished his profane existence, the merely personal ego, at the same time greatly magnified his Jewish soul. But more than this, in Rebbe Schneerson, didn't his new family also give him back his dead but perfect father? Didn't it give him back the opportunity to be the perfect son?

My pity, however, immediately turned to scorn when Billy began extolling Rebbe Schneerson's supernatural powers. He was telling me how the rebbe, being more pious than others and therefore closer to God, can work miracles through prayer. Billy knew of several people—a woman with breast cancer, a couple unable to conceive a child, a father whose son was straying from the faith—who, after asking the rebbe to intercede with God on their behalf, had soon found that their problems had been miraculously solved: the woman's cancer went into remission, the couple conceived, and the prodigal son came back into the fold.

"Billy," I said.

"Shlomo, please," he interrupted.

"Okay, Shlomo. You gotta be joking. I mean, you make the rebbe sound like Jim Jones." I knew as soon as I had said it that the comparison was unfair. But as I mentioned earlier, Jones and his deluded followers had only recently imbibed their Dixie cups of poison Kool-Aid. I wanted to dramatize to Billy how irrational and superstitious he was being, how dangerous it was to deify a man. I quoted Montaigne's famous line about puritanical zeal: "They want to get out of themselves and escape from the man. That is madness: instead of turning into angels, they change into beasts." "How can you say such a thing?" was all he said, more wounded than offended. I stammered something back about the arrogance of thinking God would take a personal interest in your problems over anybody else's. What about the starving children in Biafra? I asked him. Did God ignore their prayers? What about the Holocaust? Didn't the Jews in Auschwitz pray? Were they punished because the rebbe wasn't there to intercede for them?

"All that shows," he said, now leaning toward me, pointing his finger like a gun directly at my temple, "is what can happen when a Jew neglects his Jewishness, when a Jew forgets."

"What are you saying, that Jews caused the Holocaust? That they deserved it?"

"Who knows why *Ha Shem,* may his name be praised, does what he does? All I'm saying is that it's no accident that the German Jews were assimilationists."

"You can't be serious," I said.

"No, Al, you, you're the one who can't be serious, living in ignorance like this . . ."

"I beg your pardon."

"Ignorance and filth. No better than a goy. Betraying your own people."

Both of us were standing now. I asked him who he thought "my people" were. I said I didn't have any "people," only individuals I loved, many of them the goys he hated. "We don't hate the *goyim,*" he said. "We even encourage Jewish women who turn out to be barren to divorce and marry goys, so they don't waste Jewish sperm." "Gosh," I sneered, "how ecumenical." He didn't come here, he said, to be insulted. He came here as a *mitzvah* to me and to my parents because I was his oldest friend, because he couldn't stand to see me ruining my life. My marriage to Carol Ann was a sin against my self, my family, the Jewish community. And he hoped that someday, sooner than later, please God, I would come to my senses and put an end to this abomination. He said he would continue to pray for me. He said he would ask the rebbe to pray for me. Since I obviously hated who I was, however, we had nothing else to say to one another. He went to the door. Then he abruptly turned around. He was holding out a dollar bill. It had been blessed by the rebbe. Take it for good luck, he said, and give away another dollar bill to charity.

That was sixteen years ago. I have not heard from Billy or spoken to him since. Six years later, though, he visited my parents with his wife, a South African Jew, and their four young children. He spoke only Yiddish with my parents. He told them that his marriage had been arranged. He and his wife became engaged, he said, after spending only an hour or so in each other's company. After the wedding they moved to South Africa, where Billy became a rabbi. He hoped that soon he and his family would be moving to Israel. He didn't ask about me, and my parents didn't offer any news. The news, however,

surely would have pleased him. Carol Ann and I broke
up a year or so after Billy's visit. Even at that time our
marriage had been on rocky ground, though I didn't
want to give Billy the satisfaction of knowing anything at
all about our problems. She hated living in America, and
I refused to live in Ireland. She missed her family, her
four sisters especially, her homesickness made more acute
by her complete dependence on me and my friends—all
of whom, of course, were writers—for what community
she had. At dinner parties, at bars, at any social functions,
she often felt ignored or condescended to. "You're
always talking shop," she'd frequently complain. "Listen,"
I'd joke back, "just be thankful we aren't gynecologists."
Carol Ann was not amused. Her loneliness made her that
much more impatient with what she called my fanatical
devotion to poetry. I worked ten hours a day, seven days
a week. Not wanting to let anything interfere with my
daytime regimen of writing and reading, I balked whenever she wanted us to do something together, just the
two of us, go somewhere, have fun, relax. God forbid.
She'd accuse me of caring more for poetry than I cared
for her, which of course was true, though I denied it.
Being with her, just living, ordinary life itself, was just a

chore for me, she'd say, an obstacle, something to get out
of the way so I could go back in good conscience to my
desk. I told her it was poetry that kept me sane, that it
was poetry that enabled me to be as loving to her as I
was. Well if that's the case, she'd say, then maybe I should
try some other form of writing, because she didn't feel
loved at all. Eventually she returned to Ireland and we
divorced.

    I also had a more amicable parting of the ways
from Yvor Winters. Around the time that Carol Ann and
I split up, I began to feel constrained by the Wintersian
injunction to "write little, do it well." To chisel every
word of every poem as if in stone became, for me at
least, a recipe for writer's block. What little I wrote,
for all my patience and persistence, turned out to be
pinched, narrow, bitten back. If not for Winters himself,
then for many of his ardent followers, writing as if Ben
Jonson were looking over their shoulder placed too great
a burden on each and every line they wrote. Meter for
them, moreover, seemed more a cage than a technique of
discovery. And whereas Winters did in fact have a lion
inside him that required caging, the poems by his epi-
gones were lion cages holding pussycats. Around this

time as well, I began to read many of the poets Winters dismissed or disapproved of: Wordsworth, Coleridge, Whitman, Williams (not just the few short lyrics Winters did admire), Eliot, and Pound, and a host of more contemporary poets who were decidedly un-Wintersian: poets like Elizabeth Bishop, C. K. Williams, Frank Bidart, James McMichael, and Robert Pinsky (the last two, ironically, were students of Winters in the early sixties). And the more I read, the more impatient I became with what I felt was Winters's moralistic austerity of taste and judgment, his finicky rankings, his violent distrust of less rational, less rigorously orchestrated ways of writing. And unlike the neoformalists who were frequently invoking Winters's name, I no longer thought that accentual-syllabic meter was the only legitimate form of verse, the only road to genuine achievement.

Over the years, I've often thought of Billy. What would we say to one another if we saw each other now? I know I'd be no less uneasy with his absolutist thinking, his fundamentalism, his ironclad assurance of divine approval for everything he and his fellow Lubavitchers think and do. His total rejection of the secular world in favor of such a narrow and repressive orthodoxy still seems bizarre in the extreme. At the same time, when I think how transient my life has been, how often in the last sixteen years I've had to move, change jobs, rebuild a new life in a new place while the centrifugal pressure of professional commitments scatters old friends and family farther and farther from me, I can't help but envy Billy the fixed attachments that pervade his life. The image of a congregation worshiping together—freed from the daily drudgeries of getting and spending, from profane worries and ambitions and petty egotisms as they fix their minds as one mind upon sacred matters, ultimate mysteries, upon being itself—is an image I find more and more attractive. Though in my imagined congregation the men are not all wearing black and the women are not segregated, no longer does this act of worship seem, as it might have once, an image of irrational superstition but of reason, to quote Wordsworth, in its most exalted mood.

I have no doubt, too, that Billy would regard my life and work as pitiably flat and empty, rudderless in the most essential ways. At the same time, maybe he would have to think that, to some extent at least, his and the rebbe's prayers on my behalf were answered. A few years

after leaving Stanford I remarried, this time to a Jew. We
are not believers. We don't keep a kosher home. We
don't observe the Sabbath. And we don't belong to any
congregation. If we follow any of the 613 *mitzvot,* it's
quite by accident. Moreover, I'm no less obsessed with
poetry than I was sixteen years ago, no less compelled to
work and study every chance I get (which isn't all that
much with two young children to take care of). But
while I'm still prone to the feeling that ordinary life is an
impediment to my real life as a writer, I have grown up
enough to know that that feeling needs to be resisted,
not indulged. I'd like to think that Billy would be
relieved to know my wife and I are eager to give our
kids a Jewish education of some kind or other, not just
to teach them something about where they came from,
who they are, but also to give them a defense against the
sound-bitten, crass, increasingly homogeneous mass dis-
tractions that pass for contemporary culture. I'd like to
think that Billy would be pleased, if not entirely satisfied, with my spiritual development. But I know that he
would not be pleased. For Billy, or rather Shlomo,
anything less than complete commitment to the rigors
of Hasidic faith, to each and every one of the 613 com-

mandments, would be more contemptible than outright heresy, a more insidious betrayal. As a Hasid, he would view my emerging but still tempered sense of Jewishness as a shamelessly self-serving way of turning the most sacred matters into sacred fripperies designed to prettify an essentially secular existence. Because he thinks that being insufficiently Jewish is to make a mockery of what it means to be a Jew, because he couldn't ever be *entirely* satisfied with how I live my life, Shlomo would not be pleased at all. Shlomo would still be praying, angrier than ever, for my lost soul.

THE LAST HAPPY OCCASION

I

The morning of the day my first child, Nat, was born, I taught Elizabeth Bishop's poem "The Weed" to a group of Brandeis University English majors. I was a visiting professor at Brandeis that fall, and my wife and I were renting a house in Wellesley. I had grown up in the Boston area and had graduated from Brandeis in 1974. And though we were a good month into the semester, the strangeness of teaching at the school I had entered as a freshman twenty years before hadn't yet worn off. The students in my class only intensified the strangeness. Brandeis is still a predominantly Jewish school. Despite their more conservative appearance—shorter hair, neater clothes—the students had the same vaguely depressed and anxious air of genius in search of recognition that my friends and I had once afflicted one another with. So on the very first day of classes when a boy arrived and looked across the table at a friend of his and said, "I'm bummed," and the friend, not even looking up from the book he was thumbing through, replied, "Yeah, me too," end of conversation, I felt less like a teacher than like an aging student who was still, two decades later, a couple of credits shy of graduating.

"The Weed" is a strange, emblematic poem about the renewal of passion and the suffering that passion inevitably brings. The speaker in her dream is drawn helplessly from the desperate sleep of stoical detachment back into the world of love and loss. "I grow," the weed declares in the closing lines, "But to divide your heart again." The figure of the weed splitting open the heart it grows from, of life erupting out of dormant ground, made it easy to assimilate the poem to my present preoccupations (my wife, after all, was four days past her due date and might any moment call to tell me that her labor had begun). So I discussed the poem in terms of birth, not the physical act of giving birth, but the emotional disruptions the birth of any love entails. I suppose on that day, given my state of mind, I'd have interpreted even "Casey at the Bat" as a birth poem. But "The Weed" did seem to speak profoundly and directly to what I was feeling at that time. In the same way that the speaker associates the renewal of love with vulnerability to pain and loss, and yet ultimately prefers that vulnerability to the loveless safety of the deadened heart, the love I already felt for my soon-to-be-born child was indistinguishable from the helplessness I felt about protecting him from what, once he was in the world, he would inevitably suffer, and that helplessness on his behalf, in turn, was likewise indistinguishable from the fear of the suffering that his suffering would inevitably mean for me.

I was so consumed with my own worries and preoccupations that I never stopped to notice whether the students followed what I was saying or merely looked on, amused or bewildered that anyone could rave like a lunatic over something as inconsequential as a poem. More so than usual, I was lost in myself that day, conducting in public my own interminable education, arguing against that incorrigible side of me that wants to live forever in a state of preemptive mourning, that wants to retreat from life, to immunize itself from life by mourning in advance whatever losses the future holds in store.

This habit of distrust and vigilance is partly a family legacy, and partly a legacy of the poetry I have loved since adolescence. That family legacy is best defined by an old joke my parents loved to tell. It may be the first joke I ever learned. A policeman pulls an old Jew from a car wreck. He lays him out along the road, cushions his head against a rolled-up coat, and asks, "Mister, Mister, are you comfortable?" And the old Jew says, "Vell, I make a good living." Like the old Jew, my relatives have had their share of accidents, and like him too they have survived and even flourished in their own way by cagily ignoring or misperceiving what they've been required to endure. Their habit has always been never to give their full assent to anything, good or bad, that happens. When confronted with the bad, to thank God it wasn't worse; and when confronted with the good, to remind themselves of what they wouldn't be so lucky next time to escape. Theirs is the outsider's vigilance, the greenhorn's wisdom: always to hold, emotionally as well as monetarily, a little something in reserve because you never know. To their way of thinking, not to look for a bit of wood to knock on at the mention of any possible good fortune is a form of sacrilege, a reckless tempting of the gods. If the Quakers quake, my people knock. Knockers is what they are, even more than Jews.

This congenital inability not to think against the current of what happens explains, I think, their passion for telling stories, which in my family means telling jokes. The pleasure my relatives have always gotten from stories (mostly Jewish ones of course) is their purest (if not their deepest) pleasure because the stories are so often little cautionary tales themselves, reminding them of all the things they fear: disease, betrayal, humiliation, death, and disaster. The good joke enables them to face the worst and at the same time turn away from it; it acknowledges the worst so thoroughly it leaves them free to laugh as if life were nothing else but laughter.

I suppose all individuals, families, and cultures express, to varying degrees, some version of the mixed mode of perception I'm describing. But it does seem that my family, and Jews in general, are especially prone to it. Like hard wiring, this emotional hedging is built into the very structure of our rituals and ceremonies. It's why, for instance, the Jewish wedding culminates with the breaking of the glass: even at our most joyful, we feel compelled to think of sorrow, of loss, of the fragility of things, partly of course to appreciate more keenly the joyousness of the occasion, but also to remind ourselves not to let down our guard entirely. It's as if we half believe that there is something deeply gentile about life itself, that joy is simply life's way of getting the drop on us.

This family legacy prepared me for the poetry I fell in love with in my late teens and early twenties, for this mixed mode of perception also typifies, I think, much of the best work of Robert Frost, E. A. Robinson, Thomas Hardy, and Emily Dickinson, the poets who became, in effect, my literary family when I went to college and began to read as an aspiring writer. The poems I memorized and repeated over to myself like mantras— poems like "The Sheaves," "Spring Pools," "Wild Nights Wild Nights," "The Self-Unseeing," and "During Wind and Rain"—thrilled me not merely for the music of the language, for the elegance and tact enacted in their making, but for the active sense of life implicit in that music, elegance, and tact, a sense of life resembling mine but in

a heightened, smarter, and more challenging way. Dickinson's or Frost's hypersensitivity to time and change, to
the corrosive energies at work within the self and the
world, appeared to answer mine. But while for me the
tragic apprehension argued for emotional retreat, for
them it argued for more complete engagement. Their
inability not to perceive, say, joy, or beauty, or domestic
pleasure, in terms of all that threatens to undo it, intensified their celebration even while it seemed to qualify it.
Complex awareness wasn't synonymous, as it was for me,
with hedging bets. If I may have seen initially only a
heightened version of myself in what they wrote, and
was thereby able to cast a literary glamour around my
own emotional timidity, eventually the more I learned to
quell the egotistical noise inside my own head and yield
my attention to the attention enacted by the poems, the
more I came to see that what they offered wasn't a com-
placent pessimism but a keener responsiveness, a larger
understanding, a fuller life. They pulled me beyond my
understanding of myself even as they seemed to mirror it.

     Halfway through the class I related to the students
what had happened four days earlier, on the due date
itself; I told this story in order to illustrate the way attach-

ments and relations—the very things without which, Aristotle tells us, life would be intolerable—put us inescapably at the mercy of what we can't control; and also, if truth be told, in order to prove (like the paranoiac in the old joke) that being terrified all the time doesn't mean that there aren't forces out there waiting to get me.

Della was taking our dog Birdy, a big, dumb, lovable golden retriever, for a walk around three in the afternoon. I was upstairs watching a football game. I heard the commotion by the front door, Della cursing, as Birdy, nails scratching the floor, slipped through her grasp and bolted out the door before she got the leash attached. I wasn't especially concerned. Lately, he'd been doing that a lot with Della, whose pregnant belly made any sort of bending over now impossibly awkward. He'd wait until she got the door propped open and then dash out for a few minutes of unleashed poking about and sniffing. Exuberant but not adventurous (qualities he no doubt gets from me), Birdy had never run away. Besides, the residential horseshoe street we lived on had hardly any traffic. By then, too, all of our neighbors knew who Birdy was and liked him, and his dopey sweetness made him a special favorite among the neighborhood kids.

With no reason to worry, it took me a moment to
realize that the ferocious roar I heard and muffled screaming weren't coming from the TV but from right outside
the house. I ran out shoeless, in my stocking feet. I
found Della on her knees in the middle of the street, still
screaming, a few feet from the snarling large dog that had
Birdy by the back of the neck, his wide jaws shaking
and pulling at the fur, ripping it open, Birdy unable to
do anything but squeal. I picked up the heavy retractable
leash that Della had apparently thrown at the dog, and
I jumped in, beating him with it on his back and
haunches, though he still held on to Birdy, growling and
tearing, until his owner came out and pulled him off.

 We'd never seen the man or the dog before. As
we'd learn later, he was our neighbors' son, house-sitting
for his vacationing parents. He had tied his dog, a huge
gray wolfish-looking creature, to a tree in the driveway,
but the rope extended all the way out to the sidewalk.
And as Birdy came by the dog attacked him. Della had
thrown herself in between the dogs before falling on her
stomach. By the time the owner had pulled his dog away,
she had gotten to her feet. She was breathing heavily, a
little woozy, but seemed unhurt. Birdy limped a few

steps and then collapsed. Blood gushed from the ugly gash on his right leg, and he was bleeding from his neck, ears, and muzzle. As I was carrying him back into the house, the man said, "Hey, buddy, we have leash laws in this town," his voice merely indignant, bearing no trace of any other feeling, not the slightest concern for what his dog had done to mine or could have done to me or Della. I turned around with Birdy in my arms, his blood all over me, my wife beside me crying now. I stared at the man a moment longer, mute with rage. If he had showed even some grudging emotional awareness of what had happened, even in the form of guilty defensiveness, I might have found something to say back to him. But he was steeled in an unassailable assurance of being in the right, wholly abstracted by the law from what he saw before him. Wholly abstracted, too, by his connection to the neighborhood, to the community. His "*we* have leash laws in *this* town" reminding us not only that the law was on his side, but that we, Della and I, were outsiders, interlopers, ignorant of how things here in Wellesley were done, and so it served us right what happened. Whether justified or not, his abstractedness provoked my own; it reduced him in my eyes to what

my parents always warned me I would find, sooner or
later, in every old-stock, bleached community like Wellesley: If I was going to be the Jew, the outsider, to him,
then to me he would be the Goy.

   A few days later he slipped a note under our door,
wishing our dog a speedy recovery and hoping Della was
all right, but reminding us again that we were legally
responsible. He then concluded oddly by asking us to
please not tell his parents about what had happened. At
the time, the note enraged me even more. The note
proved, I remember telling Della, that the guy was an
unmitigated asshole, a total dickhead, he didn't deserve to
live. And yet in the weeks and months that followed, as I
told and retold the story to various friends and acquain-
tances, it was, I realize now, that note that got me
thinking about the man. That one chink in his legalistic
armor, that one faint venial whiff of fear about his parents finding out, made me, even despite myself, begin to
speculate about the larger context of experience that may
have predisposed him to react the way he did. As if it
were a poem I were writing, in the telling of the story I
found myself imagining past the various abstractions to
which we both reduced each other in the experience

itself. A young man in his early twenties, maybe he'd had
a history of trouble of one kind or another, unable to
hold down a job or form any sort of lasting attachment
to anything or anyone. Maybe this wasn't the first time
his dog had done this sort of thing, maybe there'd been
other incidents, complaints from other neighbors, a
police citation, an angry confrontation with his parents,
his parents urging him to get rid of the dog once and for
all, the son resisting, partly to irritate his parents, to assert
his independence and at the same time to prove them
wrong: he wasn't a fuckup, he could handle the respon-
sibility, the dog by then an extension of himself, of his
own unruliness. And so maybe when he faced me on the
street that day, he felt that to acknowledge what the dog
had done would be to acknowledge his own failure, to
lose the battle he'd been waging with his parents since
his early teens.

Freed from the tyranny of sheer event, from the
pressure of immediate feeling and the unconscious and
semiconscious history that feeling bears, the contemplative field I enter when I write about this man now, and
that you enter when you read about him, affords us both
a latitude of response and attention not available in the

experience itself. This contemplative field enables us to cultivate what Wayne Booth calls an upward hypocrisy, pretending to more sympathetic understanding than we ordinarily have. It enables us to enter into the inner world of people we might shun or dismiss in the normal course of our nonreading lives. This is the value of imaginative contemplation (literary or otherwise), and its limitation. I have no doubt that I'd react in similar ways if another dog attacked or threatened my wife or child or dog, and all the owner did was hide behind the legal code. How could I not? But I'd like to think that the imaginative work of writing this, of telling and retelling this story over the years, will bring me sooner to a more inclusive, more flexible grasp of the experience. On the other hand, it took me long enough to get there in relation to this man, and this was a fairly trivial incident that could have been much worse but thank God wasn't. Though we didn't know this at the time, Della wasn't hurt, there was no damage to the baby, and Birdy, badly injured though he was, would be okay after minor surgery and a two-week stay in a local animal hospital. It's no measure of my generosity of spirit that eventually I was able to think about this guy without wanting to perform a host of tortures on the most sensitive parts of his anatomy. But what if Della had been injured and we'd lost the baby? What if Birdy had been killed?

These questions, morbid as they are, make me wonder about situations even more extreme, experiences so devastating in their effects that they permanently destroy the victim's desire to understand the victimizer. Does the empathic power of imagination in which I place such faith have any power over Serbs and Muslims, Palestinians and Jews? over victims of rape? of torture? It's one thing for Homer, hundreds of years after the event, to sing with equal sympathy for Greeks and Trojans, and quite another thing for Andromache to see the complex and ultimately forgivable humanity of the soldier who hurls her small son, Astyanax, from the ramparts of Troy. Seeing this, she wouldn't lose her need for song, but the states of feeling left to her would probably confine the songs she'd want to hear to those of grief and bloodlust. How often have I told my students that to write or read poetry you have to have sympathy even for the devil. Yet now I wonder if such sympathy is only possible for those whom the devil hasn't really touched.

Only those who aren't in peril or in pain can have

the luxury of wondering about the inner lives of other
people; only those inhabiting, to some degree or other, a
zone of emotional as well as physical well-being can exercise the curiosity so essential to a fully conscious moral
life. Perhaps this is why in the *Odyssey,* the great stories
are always sung at feasts and banquets; only after the audi-
tors "have put away their desire for eating and drinking"
are they prepared to hear the bard. In this light, one
measure of a culture's moral health may be the degree to
which the culture makes available to all its people the
material comforts that the empathic power of imagination presupposes. As Bertolt Brecht once wrote, Meat
first, then ethics. While I do believe profoundly in the
power of literature to change our lives, to carry us, incre-
mentally, beyond the simplifying habits of perception to
which our history and temperament predispose us, moral
refinement is not and never could be immune to the
brutalizing effects of circumstance. And even in the best of
circumstances, things can happen that eclipse our willing-
ness, much less our power, to enter sympathetically into
other minds and hearts. It may be, too, that the openness
and receptivity entailed by moral curiosity are themselves
a form of risk, heightening our vulnerability to the very

things that can destroy the zone of comfort and well-
being that made such curiosity possible in the first place.

It wasn't until after one A.M. on Monday that we
finally got to bed. We'd spent several hours at an animal
hospital in Acton, a good hour away (the only one open
on that Sunday afternoon). The vet sent us home with
Birdy; in the morning we'd check him into an animal
hospital closer to home. His ears, neck, and leg were
shaved, and he had to wear a large ungainly Elizabethan-
like collar to keep him from licking his many wounds.
He looked ridiculous, somehow prim and clownish at
the same time, with his half-shaved muzzle drooping
through the stiff white collar, like a sixteenth-century
emblem of the disfiguring effects of pride upon our
human lineaments. The collar disoriented him completely, making it difficult for him to walk, or even
move. He'd sort of list over to a corner of the kitchen
and just stand there, his back to us, the collar brushing
the adjacent walls, the confined space apparently consoling him, as if he'd found the one place in the world that
was safe from danger. There we left him, and there we
found him several hours later, in the exact spot, when we
returned from the hospital where Della, bruised and

achy, had had a stress test to make sure the baby was all right. Before I fell asleep, I remember, I looked at the clock and thought with relief that the due date had come and gone. My son not even born yet was already showing unmistakable signs of being just like his father. He too wasn't ready for the world.

II

When I got home from classes, about five that afternoon, Della wanted to take a short walk to the Wellesley Market for a magazine. Earlier in the day, she had begun to feel a little queasy and out of sorts, and by four o'clock the contractions had clearly started. When I arrived they were still too far apart to justify any sort of panic. In her at least. I wanted to head directly to the hospital. I had visions of her collapsing and giving birth right there on Aisle Three, among the *Better Homes and Gardens.* Let me go myself, or drive you, I pleaded, but she insisted that the walk would do her good. Besides, the midwife said it might be hours yet before she'd even need to think about the hospital. So off we went, Della somehow cool and giddy at the same time, me about to enter cardiac arrest.

Halfway there we had to turn around. The contractions suddenly grew more intense and frequent. Della
could hardly walk. At one point she buckled over, her
two hands in a choke hold on a parking meter, her head
between her arms. When the pain passed, she straight-
ened up and smiled, and we walked on until the next
contraction, which I was measuring in steps now, not
minutes, from parking meter to parking meter. When we
got back to the house, Della called the midwife, who
said we could come to the hospital if we wanted but the
doctor would most likely just send us home again. Just
relax, get into a warm bath, and pour yourself a glass of
wine, she said.

I think the midwife was misled by Della's voice.
Della is a professor of Performance Studies, a discipline
within the field of Communication Studies. Although
her own work over the years has centered on scholarly
research, she has had a good deal of theatrical training
and experience. In general, apart from her professional
training, she's always been someone who engages the
world dramatistically, that is, by pretending to know
whatever it is she wants to learn before she actually
learns it. This is why she's very good at languages. She

has no compunction about mimicking the sounds of a language she doesn't know, of acting out the sense no matter how foolish it makes her seem. I, on the other hand, have no dramatic flair at all, no tolerance for humiliation, which is why I have no gift for languages.

A few years earlier, for instance, we went to France for several months. I enrolled in an eight-week language course in Aix-en-Provence. While I attended classes six hours a day, Della wandered everywhere around the town, talking to shopkeepers, waiters, old ladies on benches, young men who tried to pick her up. By the end of the summer, I was still saying things like "Madweasel" and "Monsewer" but she was practically fluent. We'd walk down the Rue Mirabeau, and people she had met would call out, "Della, Della, comment ça va?" and they'd chat like old friends while I, for all my diligence and training, stood by in utter incomprehension, stammering out (when spoken to) a few pathetic syllables, like the French equivalent of Porky Pig. Shortly after the course had ended and we'd gone up to Paris, a man approached us in the Luxembourg Gardens and asked me for a match. I actually understood his question (this was progress), and I could even see in my mind's eye the words I was supposed to say in return: "Je n'en ai pas"—No, I don't have any. What came out, though, was "M-m-merci Madame." The man of course cracked up. Della, kindhearted person that she is, sincerely tried hard not to, but did.

Della, I should add, for all her theatricality and gregariousness, is still a very private person. She's very good at using her control of voice and gift for mimicry to cover up any feeling about which she's in any way self-conscious. Talking to strangers, especially in moments of stress, she almost automatically assumes a more poised and self-possessed demeanor.

As she described her symptoms to the midwife, it drove me crazy how calm, how utterly free of pain or anxiety she seemed, unconsciously adopting a midwife's measured tone of professional concern: yes, the contractions were a little stronger now, a little more uncomfortable, no, her water hadn't broken yet, no, she hadn't vomited, wasn't really all that queasy. Just one birth pro to another, cool, calm, collected. Then as soon as she hung up, groaning out in abject misery.

Once I got Della settled in a warm bath, as the midwife had suggested, pillow behind her head, glass in hand, she vomited all over everything. Even Della now realized it was time to go.

A good thing, too, for at the hospital, we discovered Della was fully dilated, the baby had dropped. The pain in her lower back was excruciating. We spent well over an hour in the Jacuzzi shower, Della leaning forward among the jets of water, her head down between her outstretched arms, her hands against the shower wall, and me fully clothed and soaking wet behind her, massaging her back, my glasses fogging up, half-blinded by the spray. In no time the muscles in my arms began to cramp up and my fingers ached, but I kept on kneading at her lower back, primarily, of course, to ease her suffering in however small a way, but also to feel to some extent an inkling of what she herself was feeling, to bridge the gulf that her extraordinary suffering opened up between us. Yet if the pain in my body enabled me to imagine I was somehow closer to the pain in hers, that real or imagined intimacy at the same time only made me that much more aware of how unbridgeable the gulf between us was. This is not to say that my being there didn't matter, or that she was wholly disconnected from me. In *Gravity and Grace,* Simone Weil compares the soul's relation to the divine to that of two prisoners in adjoining cells, attempting to communicate through the concrete wall that separates them. What separates them, she says, also provides their only mode of communication. "Every separation is a link." Della's awareness of me came and went with the contractions. But it was easier to endure the pain, to bear the isolation the pain imposed, because she knew that I'd be there to greet her when the pain subsided. The intimacy of our connection was actually more intense for being intermittent and attenuated. And this was perhaps, at least for me, the strangest thing about the whole experience: that we had simultaneously never felt so close to one another, nor so estranged.

The nature of her suffering, though, was unlike any suffering I'd ever seen before. Not because of its intensity, or depth, for I'd seen grandparents, aunts, uncles, cousins, and friends suffer the damaging effects of strokes, of heart disease, of cancer. But what distinguished this suffering from theirs was the ferocious will it summoned up in Della. Hers was an active, not a passive suffering. The force she answered each contraction with, especially in the last stages of delivery, reclining on the bed, wailing now, now silent with the strain of pushing, her face unrecognizable, wrenched tight as rope, was so unflinching, so absolute and total, that the force hardly seemed like hers—more animal than human, more mineral than animal, as if she'd somehow drawn it up from the middle of the earth.

Later that night, long after the birth, after I cut the rubbery umbilical cord, and the cheesy blood-smeared baby rested briefly on his mother's belly, after the brief but intense terror of the neonatologist whisking him away for tests to see if there were any complications from the meconium discovered in the amniotic fluid, and after Della had been stitched back up (it took the doctor over an hour to do this) and the room was cleaned (the nurse said it looked like a slaughterhouse), with Della now asleep beside me, and the baby sleeping in my arms, half asleep myself I found myself reciting to him a lullaby by Janet Lewis:

> Lullee, lullay,
> I could not love thee more
> If thou wast Christ the King.
> Now tell me, how did Mary know
> That in her womb should sleep and grow
> The Lord of everything?

Lullee, lullay,
An angel stood with her
Who said, "That which doth stir
Like summer in thy side
Shall save the world from sin.
Then stable, hall and inn
Shall cherish Christmas-tide."

Lullee, lullay,
And so it was that Day.
And did she love Him more
Because an angel came
To prophesy His name?
Ah no, not so,
She could not love him more,
But loved Him just the same.
Lullee, lullay.

I had always loved this poem, its quiet but unmistakable orchestration of tone and argument, the marvelous turn in the last stanza, the indivisible blend of wit and profoundest feeling it expresses. But saying it over to my own child I had the strangest sense that it was reading me, that I, my soul, was being sounded by the words I chanted. No angel's prophecy could possibly enhance the love I felt for Nat, for his very being. And what the poem told me was that I was not alone in this; in feeling this I was not unlike Mary, or Janet Lewis herself, or any woman or man who holds his or her baby for the first time; which also meant I was not unlike any tyrant's parent, or any torturer's. As I intoned its lines, the poem told me this was only ordinary, and that nothing was ordinary.

As I lay there with my wife and child, I knew a wonderful adventure was beginning, wonderful in the radical sense of "full of wonder." The way a room closed up for years is utterly changed when the shade is drawn back, the window raised, I felt exhilarated and disoriented, as if my soul too suddenly had opened up to all the elements.

III

Nobody in my family has ever dropped dead telling a story or listening to one. Nobody has ever gotten sick, or if sick ever seemed so, talking at the dinner table on holidays or on more casual occasions. I knew from earliest childhood that these people weren't especially happy, that they were prone to all the various boredoms, resentments, dissatisfactions, anxieties, and grievances of people who married young (my mother was eighteen), lived

through a depression and a world war, and prospered
enough to feel real comfort but not enough to think
their comfort could ever be secure; yet all of that would
somehow fall away like a flimsy covering once they had
entered the magic circle of jokes and kibitzing. That
magic circle was the closest thing they had to Lourdes. It
didn't matter that the content of so much of what they
said had to do with troubles of one kind or another, with
illnesses and accidents, deaths and betrayals, for the very
act of telling stories seemed to insulate them from the
bad news they would talk about. It's what Bishop means,
I think, when she describes the grandparents' voices in
"The Moose" as "talking in Eternity"—not the Eternity
of memory, of the persistence of those old folks in the
poet's mind, but the Eternity they confer upon themselves, "Talking the way they talked / in the old
featherbed, / peacefully, on and on. . . ." Talking of
"Deaths, deaths and sicknesses," they nonetheless enter,
by virtue of the talk, a kind of blessed state beyond the
reach of time.

I remember thinking with a child's impeccable
logic that so long as the elders kept on talking nothing
bad could ever really touch them. And if nothing bad

could touch them, then nothing bad could touch me either.

Wasn't that what made me happy in their presence, the doubled sense of protection I could feel, for the elders formed the roof of the family house in which I had my being. I was safe so long as they were, and if the stories shielded them in turn, provided another roof over the roof they made for me, then I was that much safer. Growing up, growing older, as the elders sicken and die away—it's as if the roof were, bit by bit, being lifted off that house. The brightness of endless space begins to reach the inner chambers, and what someone else might possibly experience as freedom, an opening up, a lightening, to me feels like a terrible exposure.

Now having brought my own child into the world, it was time to make for him what my family had made for me. Time to open myself up to all the elements. Like a roof now, not like a window, to shield him from the elements by taking the elements upon me until his time comes to do the same.

Some such feelings took possession of me the day the family, those who still lived in Boston, and those who came in from elsewhere, gathered at our house in Welles-

ley for Nathaniel's *bris,* the circumcision and naming
ceremony eight days after he was born. Many of them I
hadn't seen since I graduated from college, or since my
wedding in Chicago five years earlier. Seeing my parents
now, my great-aunts Ann and Tilly, my uncle Burt, my
father's sister Ethel, my mother's cousins, Herb and
Edith, and various family friends, it was impossible not to
think of other aunts and uncles, cousins and friends who
had died in the intervening years, to feel their absence in
the presence of the people now before me.

And how changed these people were from the
people I remembered. For the better part of my childhood and adolescence they had existed for me, and in
my memory still existed, in what the writer D. R. Mac-
Donald has called "a prolonged state of elderly good
health." What ailments they had had while I was growing up—gout, high blood pressure, ulcers, and dia-
betes—some very serious, I know now—seemed in
those days to be merely a pretext for the grousing they
enjoyed so much whenever they got together. All of
them now, though, were in various stages of infirmity.
Everything about them said that they were frail and old.

Because of this, almost as soon as he arrived, Herb

took me aside to thank me for having the *bris*. "You know," he said, "this'll probably be the last happy occasion that brings all of us together. From now on, it'll be mostly funerals."

Uncle Burt was the most shockingly infirm. In his mid-eighties, his face inert, shapeless, his eyes disoriented from a recent stroke, his gait more a toddler's than a man's, he clung all afternoon to my Aunt Ann's arm as if that alone protected him from the panic he seemed always on the verge of falling into. In the old days he was a butcher, part clown, part rabbi, the family authority on the most arcane points of religious lore and ritual, and yet the sort of man who could move quickly and with no sense of dissonance from the sacred to the smutty. At a cookout at his home in Nantasket Beach the summer of my freshman year in college, while barbecuing hot dogs he asked me if I was, you know, getting any. Since at the time I wasn't, I tried finessing the question, saying there wasn't anyone I was serious about at the moment. "Serious?" he said. "What do you care from serious?" "Well, Uncle Burt, the Buddhists say it's bad karma to sleep with a woman you don't love." "Oh, they do, do they," and to emphasize his point he stuck his fork through a hot dog and jiggled it before me. "All I can tell you, Mr. Brandeis, is that bad karma's better than no karma at all."

Around that time word got out in the family that I was writing poetry, so at every gathering Burt at some point would take me by the arm and announce to everyone, "You gotta watch what you say around this guy, it's liable to end up in a little odey."

Everyone was here to celebrate Nathaniel's birth. Yet as I stood among the family, hearing again the voices I had heard since my own infancy, schmoozing, gossiping, exchanging news, it seemed that the real object of celebration was the family itself, that the *bris* was just a pretext for old friends and family to re-create themselves to themselves, to perform themselves as still belonging to each other. Here was my father explaining to Sam Winston, his old friend and colleague from their years together in the men's department at Saks, why he wished he hadn't sold the house in Brookline when he did.

"If I'd only waited another month, another month I'm telling you, for that house I coulda got three hundred and seventy-five thou, not a penny less."

"Coulda, woulda, shoulda," Sam offers wisely.

"I'm tellin' you, Sam, the day we passed papers the market it went through the roof."

"You got your health, Curls. You're living in God's country out there in California, you know, I don't have to tell you, the weather and all that."

"Yeah, yeah, the weather. It's wonderful. Wonderful. Hey, listen, it's ancient history, water under the bridge. I'm happy. We're happy. Everybody's happy. But if I only waited, Sam, no kidding, three hundred and seventy-five grand, I'm telling you, not a penny less. . . ."

Nearby, meanwhile, my mother was telling her cousin Sonny how of all her children she never thought I'd ever marry a Jew, "not my Alan. Until he's thirty, you put my Alan in a room with ninety-nine Jews and one gentile, he'll find the gentile. . . ." Then Sonny tells her about her nephew's fiancée, "Oh the personality on that girl is not to be believed, she effervesces, she positively bubbles. . . ." Which somehow reminds them of Pearl So-and-so's husband, Sidney, who died last month, my mother glancing darkly at my father as she says, "That Sidney, he couldn't do enough for Pearl, may his soul rest in peace, he served her hand and foot. He couldn't *think* of enough ways to make her happy. . . ."

The almost Homeric epithets, the clichés and formulaic phrases, the familiar gestures and intonations, a kind of abrasive call and response, pushing and inviting

to be pushed back in turn—"So, Mr. Fancy Pants,"
"What a bunch of bums," "It wasn't meant to be," "Listen, at least you got your health," "May you live and
be well"—seemed to acknowledge time and to resist it,
converting anything that happened, sorrow, joy, or
disappointment, into a kind of tribal cadence that said,
despite the "deaths, deaths and sicknesses," that nothing
had really changed.

 If Eternity for the old folks on the bus in Bishop's
poem is "Talking the way they talked / in the old
featherbed, / peacefully, on and on, / dim lamplight in
the hall, / down in the kitchen, the dog / tucked in her
shawl . . . ," for my relatives it's talking the way they talk
around a tray of cold cuts.

 Eternity is a sacred affair (preferably catered), but
not especially solemn, for these are not religious people.
They go to synagogue (mostly Reform) only on the
High Holidays, or on the anniversary of the death of a
parent, wife, or husband to say *Kaddish*. They fast on
Yom Kippur, they eat unleavened bread during Passover,
but few of them keep kosher. They were all anxious to
give their children a religious education, though they
themselves had none. While they would have preferred

that their children marry in the faith, they'd long since by necessity made their peace with the social/sexual mores of their baby-boomer kids. And while they believe in the God of their fathers, that God is less an active presence in their daily lives than the last line of defense against catastrophe.

For these people the object of celebration is always the family. And the family is never more aware of itself as family than when it's telling stories. They dutifully attended to the prayers the *mohel* intoned, the circumcision and the benediction afterward. But as soon as he concluded and the last Amens were said and he was out the door, they gathered themselves into a circle for the main event, the unofficial but more important ceremony that would show Nat what it meant to be a member of the tribe.

As always, my Great-Aunt Ann presided. Not because she's an especially good storyteller but because she knows more stories than anybody else. She's always been the family archivist of stories, the one to whom everyone defers. Burt, her husband, was so proud of this place of honor she occupied that he spent the last years of his life painstakingly transcribing all the jokes she knows on index cards, to make it easier for her to remember them after he was gone. The year after he died, she got the cards out to show me. There were hundreds of them. In a minuscule trembling script, remarkably legible given his age and various infirmities, he covered every square inch of every card, front and back, with jokes in English and Yiddish. Next to each punch line, he'd put the date and initials of the person who first told the joke, or the occasion at which Ann first told it: "Susan's wedding, 1974," "Jimmy's Bar Mitzvah, 1957." It was as if each joke were a picture in a family album, the memory device by which, despite his failing body, he vigilantly kept his past alive.

Ann also knew better than anyone else which people told which jokes best. It was a violation of decorum to tell a story that belonged to someone else by virtue of his or her gift for telling it. So, for instance, when in honor of Nat, my mother asked her to tell the one about the Japanese rabbi—he's fired from his congregation for performing circumcisions karate-style—Ann declined because that was Jimmy's story, and he wasn't there. "Nobody tells that story the way Jimmy does."

In the fourth book of the *Odyssey,* after Helen and

Menelaus feed Telemachus and exchange news about
each other's lives, Helen entertains her young guest by
telling him a story of his father, Odysseus, at Troy. Before
she tells the story, though, she laces Telemachus' wine
with a magic potion given to her in Egypt, a potion capable of making one "forget all sorrows, and whoever had
drunk it down would have no tear roll down his face,
not if his mother died and his father died, not if men
murdered a brother or a beloved son in his presence. . . ."
Now Telemachus can hear a story about his missing
father without pain and grief preventing him from receiv-
ing what the story has to give. All arts, however realistic
they appear, employ enchantment of one kind or
another. In the case of poetry, or really any verbal art,
including telling jokes, "Egyptian medicine" is provided
by the physical shape and patterns of unfolding form as
they reveal themselves in sentence, cadence, figures of
thought or speech. That sensuous formal pressure trans-
forms the reality it appears to bring so directly into focus.
By converting the materials of life into the terms of art
(much as Perseus defeats Medusa by converting her into
an image on his shield), it enables the audience to experience as pleasure what in actuality would be too painful

to confront directly. If the transformation grows too great, the stylization too extreme, and the counterpressure of reality no longer challenges the pressure of the form, the performance degenerates into self-applauding triviality, the enchantment into boredom. But if the transformation isn't great enough, as it so often isn't in the so-called "naked poetry" of demotic self-disclosure and sincerity, we grow just as bored, if not disgusted.

In comparing jokes with poetry, or literature in general, I don't mean to suggest that jokes perform the same sort of moral inquisitiveness that I believe is central to the literary arts. Far from disrupting entrenched perceptions, most jokes reinforce cultural values and stereotypes. But like the formal elements of poetry or fiction, or, for that matter, essays like this one, the rhetorical devices a good joke brings into play—hyperbole, bathos, pun, timing of voice, plot turns of one kind or another—transform into pleasure experiences that otherwise would terrify or repel. The range of experiences in the jokes my relatives told that afternoon—the miseries of old age, death, disappointment, impotence, to name a few—reflected their worst fears and anxieties. And insofar as the stories enchanted those fears and anxie-

ties into laughter, they overcame them, or held them at
bay, at least for the duration of the telling.

Aunt Ann began by telling a family favorite. A
rabbi, a minister, and a priest are talking about how
they'd each like to die. The minister says he'd like to die
peacefully in his sleep. The priest says he'd like to die in
a plane crash, so that maybe he could give the Last Rites
to a fellow passenger before they hit the ground. The
rabbi says, "Vell, vhen I die, I should suffer, and linger,
and suffer, and linger, and then get better."

After college, I went to Ireland for a year. There I
learned the hard way how much a good joke depends on
context for its effect, that the humor resides less in the
joke's intrinsic properties than in whom it's told to, and
when it's told. This is also true of poetry, to some extent.
A limerick, or a short poem by Ogden Nash, is probably
more appropriate as an after-dinner toast at a bachelor
party than a passage from *Paradise Lost*. Anyway, I was the
best man at a friend's wedding in Dublin. After the ceremony, the wedding party adjourned to a nearby pub, and
after a while people started telling jokes. Eventually it
was my turn. Since at the time I knew mostly Jewish
jokes (I had after all just graduated from Brandeis), I told

this one, thinking funny is funny, no matter where you are. I'd knocked back a few pints by then, so I really laid on the Yiddish, I schmaltzed it up as best I could, drawing out the "er" on *suffer* and *linger,* a whole race's worth, five thousand years of heartache in my voice. Nobody laughed. The father of the bride leaned over to the groom and said, "Now why's yer man there talkin' in that queer voice?"

Ann then told the one about the Jew in *shul.* He's praying, "Please, God, let me win the lottery. My whole life I've been a good Jew, I keep a kosher home, I go to *shul,* I don't drink, I don't cheat on my wife, I work hard, and yet I can't make a buck, I don't have two cents to my name, while my brother, Morris, gambles and whores, he profanes the Sabbath, he beats his wife, and yet everything he touches turns to gold. Why, God, why can't I for once in my life win the lottery? Would it be so terrible?" And a voice booms down out of the heavens, "'Why, Lord, why?'—because you're such a *nudzh,* that's why!"

A few years later the same friend at whose wedding I was best man told me the Irish version of the same joke. In church Seamus is praying the same prayer, he's a good Christian, a loving family man, a hard worker, yet he can't make ends meet, while his brother Sean the drunkard is a millionaire ten times over. Why, God, why? And a fist bursts through the roof of the church and nails him against the pew, and the voice says, "'Cause I fookin' hate ya!"

Had I known this version of the story at the time I don't think I would have told it. At these sessions I'm a child again. Only the grown-ups get to speak. As they went around the room, now my mother telling a couple of stories, now Sam Winston, Ethel, then Ann again, and then my mother, I realized that as a child especially, the pleasure I felt among them wasn't only from the sense of protection that I mentioned earlier, but also from the almost privileged invisibility conferred upon me by their absorption in each other. I got to see them as they really were, divested of parental dignity, their guard down, the proprieties suspended, using a language they never used at home, except perhaps at times of crisis, talking among the children as if the children weren't there. I know now, of course, that it wasn't who they really were that I was seeing then, but who they got to be at such times. It was a privileged space they'd entered, a space that not only

seemed to insulate them from unhappiness but also per-
mitted a freedom of manner and expressiveness nowhere
else available to them. As a child, I studied them on these
occasions as if they were the text of what it meant to be
a grown-up, as if the sometimes frightful, harried,
unyielding, and impatient ways they usually were were
simply how they thought they had to act before their
children. Now I know otherwise. The text is just a count-
ertext, sealed off like a ritual observance, like the sacred
itself, from the ordinary difficulties of profane existence.
I had no doubt that the storytelling ritual renewed their
sense of who they were together as a family, and that it
turned trouble and insecurity and fear, and even their
daily moralisms, into an amoral but triumphant pleasure.
But I also knew that that family sense, because it has to
be enacted to be really felt, because it's something they
do, not something they are, would not outlast the afternoon, or if it did outlast it, would not protect them from
so many of the very things they joked about that day.

Throughout the storytelling, Nat celebrated his
official status as Jew and family member by sleeping
soundly by my side in the portable car seat that the *mohel*
had renamed the Chair of Elijah (the prophet Elijah is

thought to be the guardian of newborns: for three days
he hovers over the infant's cradle, warding away any and
all evil spirits). Elijah's presence notwithstanding, all afternoon I fussed at the baby's blanket, wrapping it around
him and rewrapping it, never satisfied that he was snug
enough against the chill of the drafty room. His being
there beside me made me think of all the other times I'd
sat like this, listening to the elders. I thought of how
remarkable it was that I was here again, back home after
nearly twenty years of wandering, a middle-class American Odysseus disguised not as a beggar, but as the next
best thing, a university professor. I thought of how
throughout my adolescence I couldn't wait to get away
from Boston, to get away from them, of how oppressed
I was by what I took to be their prejudices and hypocri-
sies, their unquestioned faith in the status quo, their
deep-seated belief that the only measure of a man's worth
is the size of his bank book, that business is truth, and
truth business, that is all ye know on earth and all ye
need to know. It was to purify myself of all I thought
they represented that I went to Ireland when I graduated
from college, to live as an expatriate poet in the land of
Yeats and Joyce, Kavannagh and Heaney, eventually even

marrying an Irish woman. I wanted to live what I imagined was the literary life, which I defined in those days negatively as everything my family wasn't. The irony was, of course, that the very poetry in whose name I rejected my own family was reminding me that in rejecting them I was rejecting life itself. It took me the better part of two decades to realize the truth of G. K. Chesterton's remarks that the "men and women who, for good reasons and bad, revolt against the family, are, for good reasons and bad, simply revolting against mankind. Aunt Elizabeth is unreasonable, like mankind. Papa is excitable, like mankind. Our youngest brother is mischievous, like mankind. Grandpapa is stupid, like the world; he is old, like the world."

Of course realizing that Grandpapa is stupid, like the world, doesn't make his stupidity any less oppressive, or the need to change the world any less urgent. If utopian dreams of social justice, universal respect, and compassion are more available to adolescents than to adults, then so much the worse for adults. Yet in seeing that the family is humdrum, like the world, is flawed, like the world, I also came to see that it is strange, like the world, that it is beautiful, like the world, especially on occasions such as these. In fact, whatever purchase I still have on that utopian dream derives in part from these storytelling sessions, even if the stories themselves at times were crude or fraught with biases. For here, if nowhere else, the family had shaken free of its habitual worries, its often stultifying respectabilities, its need to keep up appearances at any cost. Here, too, if nowhere else, they were at ease with one another, the women and men on equal footing, delighting in each other, according each other mutual respect and recognition. "Sam, tell the one about the tattoo on the penis. . . ." "Marilyn, tell that French one, you know, the 'probably' joke, nobody can tell that one like you. . . ." Implicit in the ritual requests and compliments, in the irreverence and laughter, is a kind of paradisal dream in which a sense of fair play and pleasure, dignity, order, and sheer anarchic foolishness, social concord and individual expressiveness, are simply different facets of a single act of communion. And even if that dream seldom or never so completely extended beyond the borders of the occasion itself, when I now imagine what a just society would look like, I imagine people such as these, telling the sorts of stories they told that afternoon, the storytelling doing for them what Eli-

jah was supposed to do for Nat, protecting them from
evil spirits, warding away anything in them or around
them that might diminish the life-affirming pleasure of
each other's company.

Ethel had just finished telling the one about the
old Jew whose wife is dying of an incurable disease. She
emerges from a coma and whispers, "A little lovemaking, please, I want a little lovemaking." So her husband
obliges, and she miraculously recovers. The family is
jubilant, but the old Jew is off in a corner crying
inconsolably. "Pa," his son asks, "what's wrong, why
aren't you happy?" And he says, "How would you feel, if
you could've saved Eleanor Roosevelt, and didn't lift a
finger?"

When the laughter died down, Ann asked me,
"So, Alan, haven't you got a story for us?" It was the first
time I'd ever been invited to participate. With the birth
of Nat, it seemed, I'd earned the right to take my place
among them, to join them in the magic circle. I don't
think I knew this at the time but the joke I told was
really on myself, or about myself, about how it felt to recognize myself as one of them. I looked around at the
family, at their welcoming attentive faces. I consigned

Nat to Elijah's care, I forgot about the draft. I forgot that several of the people I was seeing I would never see again once the afternoon was over. And forgetting all of this, I joined them in their eternity, which was my eternity now. A Jew, a Frenchman, and a German are ship-wrecked on a desert island. After twenty years, a lamp washes ashore, and when they rub it a genie appears who gives them each one wish. "I wish," the Frenchman says, "to be home in Paris making passionate love to my beautiful mistress Claudette." Poof, he's gone. "I wish," says the German, "to be home in Berlin making love to my wife Hildebrande." And poof, he's gone too. The Jew, looking around him, says, "I'm kind of lonely now without those guys. I wish they were here with me."

SITTIN' IN A FUNERAL PLACE

As Russ and I put on our masks, our rubber gloves, our
yellow hospital gowns, our paper caps and slippers, he
warned me not to be too shocked at how my sister
looked. The amount of chemotherapy involved in the
stem cell transplant was much higher than in any of her
previous treatments, and those had devastated her. What
the poison is designed to do, he said, is kill her as much
as possible without killing her off, and he thought the
doctors might have overdone it and brought her closer to
the brink of death than they intended because she'd been

running a high fever for several days now, had nonstop vomiting and diarrhea, and her mouth and throat were one big open wound, one continuous canker sore extending all the way down to her esophagus.

As I slipped the mask on, Russ advised me to press the top part over the bridge of my nose. "That way," he said, already an old hand at this, "your glasses won't fog up when you breathe."

Beth could hardly turn her head in our direction as we entered. Her face was drawn and pale, a kind of chalky yellow, and her hair, which had only just begun to grow back from her earlier chemotherapy and in a few days would fall out again, was much grayer than it was before her illness.

"Thanks for coming to help out, Al," she murmured.

"Hey, Houston in July, what's not to like."

She started to smile, then caught herself, saying it hurt her mouth too much to laugh. She was wearing a loose-fitting nightgown unbuttoned at the top, and when she propped herself up on one elbow to take a sip of water, the gown hung open to expose the jagged scar from the mastectomy. Before I glanced away, it struck me

that I was staring, unembarrassed and unrepulsed, at a
part of her body I would have quickly looked away from
had the breast been there. Beth, however, was far too
gone in her own pain to care what anybody saw. Normally, Russ had told me, Beth refused to go out in public
without her wig, and even at home, she'd wear a turban
or headdress of some kind or other to cover up her bald-
ness. That self-consciousness, however, had vaporized
before the onslaught of her present suffering. Matter-of-
factly, she told Russ that he would have to bring her a
few more nightgowns because she'd already soiled the
ones he'd brought her yesterday. In passing, she described
her "accidents," how frequently she has to go yet how
impossible it is to get herself up out of bed in time, and
how impatient the night nurse is that she refuses to use
a bedpan. I tried imagining her at the most degrading
moments, shivering while the night nurse sponges her
down, remakes her bed, and cleans the floor. I imagined
her at such times thinking about her daughter, Gabbi, or
her job as director of a university library, or her home,
her bedroom, her most cherished things, her mind trying
to pull away from the gravitational force of the painful and
humiliating present to remind herself who she really is.

Yet the more I listened to her, the more I realized how wrong that image of her was. Like a jealous daughter, her body would have let her think of almost nothing but itself. As I listened to her talk about these accidents as one might talk about the news or weather, I realized that was what her body was now, news and weather; the world, with all her interests and affiliations, passions and obligations, contracted to her burning mouth and anus, her blood count, her nausea. Which is not to say that she had lost her sense of dignity, for dignity, like pleasure, is relative to what the terms of life allow at any given moment. Her suffering had forced her temporarily to redraw the boundaries of her dignity, to shift it from its outward bodily manifestations onto something less dependent on what she couldn't now control. By refusing to use the bedpan, by lowering the guardrail of her bed, despite the doctor's insistence that she keep it raised, and by talking about her body as if it were something wholly outside herself, some external matter of disinterested concern, even while it absorbed every ounce of her attention, she preserved what freedom, dignity, and personal autonomy she could find within such narrow straits.

Though Beth would no doubt hate the compari-

son, in this respect she reminded me of Nana, our
grandmother, who had come to live with us in 1962
when I was ten and Beth was sixteen. Though only sixty
at the time, Nana seemed ancient. She'd already had
three strokes by then, her first in 1948. She was terribly
overweight and toddled like a two-year-old, her face partially paralyzed and her speech slurred. Before her illness,
she'd been highly successful, had made a small fortune
retailing women's clothing. She divorced her first husband when my mother was three and left her with
her parents in order to devote herself to her flourishing
business. She was a proud, impatient, and combative woman who didn't suffer fools gladly, and she assumed that
everyone around her was a fool till proven otherwise.
Her various infirmities only exaggerated her contempt
for others. She especially hated being dependent on my
mother. She regarded as insult the care she knew she
couldn't live without, and seemed to make up for the degradation of her neediness with ridicule and criticism.
Often my mother would have to leave work early to run
the many errands Nana would routinely send her on, and
if she forgot to get the mouthwash she had asked for, or
her dietary candy, or the cigarettes, Nana would call her

"Party Girl," "Princess," "Madam Butterfly." "God forbid," she would say, "you should think of anyone but yourself." From time to time, my mother would blow her top, but mostly she suffered the daily carping and abuse in silence. It almost seemed to make her that much more devoted to her mother, that much more determined to do for her mother and, by doing, to remind her mother of what she had never done for her. Being the perfect daughter may have been the best revenge.

I was the only member of the family who was spared Nana's wrath. In a way we were thrown together. My sister and brother were teenagers by then and were hardly ever home. Plus, being teenagers and extremely sensitive to differences of any kind, they were too embarrassed by her obesity, incontinence, and overall cantankerousness to ever bring their friends around, and they resented her for this. My parents were preoccupied with making ends meet as well as with the strain my grandmother's presence placed on an already shaky marriage. So Nana and I were often alone together. And seeing in each other an image of our own powerlessness, we became co-conspirators against the family order. She would let me sneak into her room after my bedtime, and we'd stay up till all hours watching Johnny Carson, old westerns, and reruns. I'd lie in her bed under the covers while Nana sat in her chair, a nimbus of cigarette smoke about her head as she reviewed the actors and entertainers in every show we'd watch, which meant she'd tell me which ones were Jewish, a category she would break down further into the saintly few like Myron Cohen, Milton Berle, Alan King, who didn't hide their Jewishness, and those like Cary Grant who did, and who were therefore no better than the Nazis. We'd memorize the jingles to commercials: "Miller High Life, the champagne of bottled beer"; "Ho ho ho, Green Giant"; "Timex: it takes a licking and keeps on ticking." Eventually, identifying jingles became a kind of game with us. All of a sudden in the middle of a show she might blurt out "Winston tastes good," and I'd sing, "like a," then she'd clap twice, before I'd sing again, "cigarette should." Sometimes she'd get weird and rail against her ex-husbands, who, she'd claim, were coming around the house during the day and stealing her money; or she'd start to cry about her sister-in-law Kitty or brother-in-law Hy, or her parents, all of whom had died some years before but whom she'd cry for now as if she'd only gotten the news that day. After a while I'd say the first line of a Burma Shave ad, "Don't lose your head to save a minute," and she'd snap out of it, saying back, on cue, "you need your head, your brains are in it," and together we'd sing, "Burma Shave!" and go on watching television as if nothing had occurred.

In return for her letting me stay up past my bedtime, I would often sneak out of the house in the early evenings to buy her the forbidden chocolate sundaes that she craved. "Alan," she'd call me, "Alan, come upstairs." Then in the mysterious voice of the C.I.A. chief in "Mission Impossible" she'd say, "Your mission, Alan, should you decide to accept it, is to go to Brighams and procure one chocolate sundae. Leave immediately. This tape will self-destruct in ten seconds."

We were also drawn together in our incontinence. Though ten years old, I still wet the bed, and so did Nana, being too heavy and slow-moving to get up in time. Often, I'd fall asleep in front of the television, she would lie down next to me, and invariably in the middle of the night we'd wake up in the wet sheets, cold and uncomfortable. In the darkness we would change our clothes, then together strip the bed and put new sheets on and go back to sleep—a little embarrassed, yes, but

mostly grateful, I now think, to have someone other than
ourselves for once to blame.

Aside from visits to the doctor, Nana only left the
house to get her hair done once a week at the corner
beauty parlor. Her hair was bleached blond and permed
up in an elaborate bouffant, which over the course of the
week would sag like a balloon slowly losing air. Though
she saw no one and went nowhere, she cared enor-
mously about her appearance, not surprising for someone
who had made her living in the fashion industry. Each
day she'd put on rouge, mascara, lipstick, do her nails,
get her hair just so, then sit before the television all day
long. Because her old life had now dwindled to these
outward trappings, she seemed to cling to them more
desperately, not to deny the truth of what she was, which
would have been impossible, but rather to remind herself
continually, despite that truth, that she was more than
this. But how else could she express that, make it visible,
except through the very body that betrayed her, as if her
body were both ally and enemy, wound and balm, the
theater in which she struggled to perform what she once
had been upon the stage of what she had become. When
I'd get home from school, I'd sometimes find her on the
kitchen floor, having slipped in a puddle of urine. "*Oy*

Gottenyu," she'd say over and over as I'd get her to her feet, and if she wasn't injured, even before she'd change her dress, she'd check her hairdo to make sure every hair was still in place, and reapply her makeup while I mopped the kitchen floor.

Beth's body seemed to change, or rather her relation to it changed, when I asked her if she'd talked with Gabbi. She'd arranged for Gabbi to go out to L.A. to stay with our mother and father for the first week of her hospitalization. The plan was for my mother to bring Gabbi back on Sunday and stay on for a week or two so that the two of us could help around the house during Beth's second week of isolation. Apparently the visit had not gone well, which was no surprise to me. My father, in his late seventies, is blind in one eye and has insomnia, my mother has terrible arthritis in her hands and back, and it's been many many years since they've taken care of children. Gabbi would be a handful for anyone at any age. She's a delightful six-year-old but is extraordinarily energetic. Beth calls her "the tornado." Her deep anxiety about her mother's illness and her general sense of disorientation from being so far from home had no doubt made her especially hard to manage. By the middle of

the visit she was calling Russ and begging him to take
her home. She said that Grandma was yelling at her
all the time, she wouldn't let her wear the clothes she
wanted, now wouldn't even kiss her goodnight. "She says
I'm making Mommy worse by not behaving," she told
her father. And when Russ passed all of this on to Beth,
she called our brother David, who also lives in Los
Angeles, and implored him, in tears, to please take her
for the remainder of the visit, which he did.

As Beth recounted all of this, her voice grew
stronger, seeming to reenter her body to draw from it
the anger she needed to defend her child against her
mother. And as she was turning toward us, her head
raised off the pillow, that anger in turn changed her body,
conjuring out of it, above and beyond her suffering, both
the maternal body full of rage and protectiveness and the
filial body full of a child's, a daughter's, longstanding
opposition to her mother. At one and the same time, she
was her mother's angry daughter and her daughter's
angry mother as she said, "I don't know what I'll tell Ma
when she gets here. I mean, she has no right to treat my
kid like that."

"She did the best she could," I said. "She's an old
lady."

"Yeah, well, she made a big show of wanting to help out. Can't even take care of a six-year-old."

"That's the way she is, Beth. That's the way she was with us," I said.

"Jesus, she's just a kid," Beth continued, as if I hadn't said a thing. "Her mother's sick. She's far from home. What does Ma expect?"

"Beth, listen: That's Ma. Nothing you can say is gonna change her."

"Well, I won't forgive her, not for this."

"You have to," I said. "You just have to eat it."

"You fight her," Russ added, "you're gonna lose."

"If I'm lucky," she said, ignoring both of us, "I'll be too sick to see her by the time she comes." Her head fell back to the pillow, her eyes closed, and she was little more now than just her suffering body, hardly anybody's mother, anybody's child.

That evening I called my mother.

"That child," she told me almost as soon as I said hello, "the mouth on her you wouldn't believe."

"Ma," I said, "she's six years old, she misses her mother. For God's sake, cut her some slack."

"None of my other grandkids talk to me that way."

"None of your other grandkids has a mother with cancer."

"This has nothing to do with that," she snapped back. "Gabbi's been fine, she hasn't been unhappy here, and Russ is a horse's ass for believing what she tells him, and he had no business repeating any of it to Beth."

"Well," I said, knowing from hard experience that these were unwinnable arguments, "what are you gonna do? They treat her like a person. They don't order her around."

"What you do mean 'like a person'? We never treated you kids like a person and you all turned out okay."

"Let it go, Ma," I said. "She's just a kid."

"So is it too much to expect a please from time to time, a thank you?"

"Ma, it's their child."

"No respect for elders. None. How do you raise a kid like that? I'm telling you, Al, I'm tempted when I bring her back to just turn around and go home and not stay at all."

"So why don't you?" I said. "You're probably worn out from taking care of her, you've done enough for Beth already. Why don't you just go home."

"I can't do that. I have to come."

"Why? Beth's in the hospital. I can take care of
Gabbi."

"Don't be silly. Who's going to cook? Clean?"

"It's not as if Russ and I have never taken care of
children."

"I have to come," she repeated. "She's my
daughter."

"But there's really nothing you can do at this
point."

"I have to."

"Well, okay, but if you're going to come, come
cheerfully. Not with a chip on your shoulder. That's the
last thing everybody needs."

"So give Beth my love," she said and hung up.

An hour later, she called back, brisk and business-
like, just to say that she had changed her ticket and
would not be staying. She almost got the phone call over
with before I realized she was taking my advice.

There were two flights from Los Angeles arriving at the
same time, and Russ and I met the wrong one. When
we caught up with Gabbi and my mother at baggage
claim, my mother seemed to grow more panicky, as if

now that we'd arrived she could allow herself to feel
what she had had to hold in check for Gabbi's benefit.
"Where the hell were you?" she asked. "Grandma said
you went to the wrong airport," Gabbi announced.
Before I could answer, Russ said, "Here, this is for you,
from me and Beth." My mother was too flustered by her
fear and anger to see the gift-wrapped box that he was
holding out to her. He had to put it in her hand. She
stared at it a moment, befuddled, not quite registering
what it was, then stuffed it in her bag, kissed Gabbi, and
as she walked off said we didn't need to wait with her,
and that was that.

At six o'clock, as we'd arranged, we stood across the
street from the hospital, looking up at Beth's third-story
window. The sun reflected off the glass, obscuring her as
she waved down at us. "Wave, Gabbi," Russ was saying,
"there's your mommy, wave to her." Gabbi squinted, one
hand shielding her eyes, the other waving. "Hi Mommy,
here I am! Can you see?"

One evening after dinner, Gabbi started to sing, "Ooh,
ooh, ooh, Miss Grace, sittin' in a funeral place, the
moment I saw your face, you know, girl, I loved you. . . ."

"Gabbi, what song is that?" I asked.

"'Miss Grace' by the Platters," she said.

"Weird lyrics, huh?"

"It's just how it goes."

"You sure?"

"Yeah, why?"

"Well, 'sittin' in a funeral place' doesn't exactly sound like a love song."

"Does to me. Anyhow, I'll prove it." And she got the tape out and played it.

"Gabbi," I said, laughing, "it's not 'sittin' in a funeral place,' it's 'satin and perfume and lace.'"

"No it isn't," she said.

"But it doesn't make any sense, your way."

"Who says?" And she danced away, happily singing, "Ooh, ooh ooh, Miss Grace, sittin' in a funeral place. . . ."

All week the final lines of Frost's "Out Out" were haunting me: "Nothing to build on there. And they, since they / Were not the one dead turned to their affairs." When I wasn't visiting Beth, or squiring Gabbi back and forth from home to horseback-riding camp, while reading or writing, or wondering how everyone at home was getting on, I'd suddenly realize that I hadn't been thinking of my sister, that she'd been wholly absent from my mind, "dead" to me for hours at a time while I turned so easily to my own affairs. Not that it would have done her any good for me to brood about her constantly. Forgetting her even for brief periods, however, made me conscious of how alone she was inside her body, how inaccessible her pain and suffering made her to even the closest kin, and how obscenely life would go on, my own, her husband's, and her daughter's, whether she was here or not.

Sealed up as we are inside our own skin, physically autonomous, we experience our bodies, nonetheless, when we are well, mostly in relation to other people. We each possess a plurality of bodies, or bodily idioms called into being by our various roles, affiliations, and commitments as brother or sister, husband or wife, son or daughter, Southern Baptist or Northern Jew, friend or neighbor. Neither fixed nor singular, our physical being is overlaid with gestural dialects, accents, and intonations peculiar to each of these relations. In health, we unthink-

ingly command these idioms. We switch continually
from this bodily code to that, or fluently speak two or
more at one and the same time, as when a father at the
market with his infant son asleep on his shoulder runs
into an old colleague he hasn't seen in months: his one
hand rubbing the baby's back while the other shakes
his friend's hand or gestures as they talk, his body simultaneously expressing father and friend, comforter and
colleague. But what in times of health is merely the physical fact about us all—our existence in separate bodies—
becomes emotionally and psychologically the truth in
times of sickness. And the more extreme the sickness,
the more alone inside our own skin we become. As the
week went on, and her blood counts continued dropping, and her suffering grew even more extreme, my
sister seemed to undergo a kind of bodily aphasia, unable
to so much as lift her head, or smile, hardly aware of
me or anyone at all. The dense array of bodily dialects at
her command had now deserted her, making her body
nothing but an echo chamber of its own distress.

"Write a poem," she had said a few weeks earlier,
before the treatment, when I called to ask what sorts of
things I could do for her when I came out. At that time
too she felt well enough to think about her illness as a

gift, for it had given her, she said, such a keen apprecia-
tion of what it meant to be alive, of all the blessings that
her life possessed. Her friends, her family, neighbors, colleagues at work, even people she assumed disliked her,
rallied around her to offer what help they could; they vol-
unteered to help take care of Gabbi, they ran errands,
they cooked meals, sent cards and flowers. Had she not
gotten sick, she said, she never would have realized how
many people loved her, how much she had to be truly
grateful for. That was before the treatment. Now, when
she talked at all, she said, Please let me die. If there was
anything giftlike in her present suffering, the suffering
would have to pass before she'd be able to see it. In its
clutches she was beyond the reach of anybody's love
or kindness, of poetry, of conversation, of relatedness of
any kind.

Gabbi seemed to have no trouble accepting Russ's expla-
nation why she couldn't visit her mother. He told her
little kids have more germs than grownups because they
play outside.

"Yeah," Gabbi had said, "and I'm around horses
all the time too, and they have *lots* of germs."

Despite the disruptions caused by her mother's

illness, Gabbi pursued her usual interests with undistractable intensity. Watching her at the stables every day as she brushed the horses down, fed them, cleaned out their stalls, and rode the gigantic creatures around the track, I thought of Keats's observation that "difficulties nerve the spirit of man—they make our prime objects a refuge as well as a passion." While I was there, she didn't cry at all, she didn't throw a single tantrum, or even ask much about her mother. Nor did she seem terribly upset when she and Russ would call Beth and Beth would be too tired or sick to talk. Whatever terror, anxiety, or grief she felt expressed itself unconsciously, in her bodily movements, in her games and interests, in the very things that simultaneously expressed her almost animal high spirits. Almost as soon as we got home in the evenings from the stables, she'd get her toy horses out and bring them to the dining room, or downstairs bathroom, or den, where she'd set up a track, near Russ or me, but never in the same room, constructing fences out of piles of books. One or two books served for the lower fences, three or four for the higher ones, and eight, always eight, for the last and highest. One by one, she'd run horses around the track. And as each fence approached, she'd say, "Now easy, girl, you can do it, easy," and slowly lift the horse up over, first the front hooves, then the back. Each horse, though, would hesitate before the daunting eight books of the last fence, would neigh and rear. Gabbi would say, "Okay, just relax now, nice and easy," then lift the horse up, the front hooves catching on the top book, sending all of them, horse and books, sprawling across the room. Then she'd pile the books back up again, say in her ever-encouraging instructor's voice, "Come on, girl, you can do it, just relax, ease into it," and run the horse back toward the fence, and knock it over, three or four times, before it finally cleared. With each of her twenty or so horses, she'd repeat the ritual until all of them had cleared the highest fence.

By Thursday, the last day of my visit, Beth was feeling better. Her blood counts had started rising, and almost as soon as they had, her mouth healed, her diarrhea let up, and her vomiting stopped, though the queasiness persisted. That morning, she called to ask me to bring over any personal mail she had received. In the pile I brought her was an official-looking letter from someone on her staff at the library. She said, "Oh God, not him, the jerk knows I'm in the hospital," and immediately called her secretary and told her to tell so-and-so to stop his goddamn whining, and that she wouldn't get around to considering his request until her sick leave was over. The IV tube was flapping against the bedside as she yelled into the phone, her anger now a measure of her returning health.

The doctor said by Saturday she'd be well enough to leave the hospital, though she'd feel debilitated and out of sorts for months to come. For a while she'd exist in that peculiar stage in her recovery in which she'd be too strong for the hospital, yet too weak for the world, able to repossess her body only enough to feel again the claims of those who loved and needed her, but not enough to feel that she could satisfy those claims. If health is a kind of animal insensitivity to the overwhelmingness of things, Beth still had a long, long way to go. She told me she was scared about returning home, worried that she wouldn't have the stamina for it. Her daughter would be all over her, insatiable in her demands and needs if only because she knew she could be, now that Beth was home. And then of course there would be

Russ, his needs, demands, desires. For much of the past
eight months he had had to be more mother than father
to his daughter, more nurse than husband to his wife.
Since the mastectomy, Beth mentioned one day (in passing and without any further comment), he had stopped
sleeping in their bedroom. Was it respect for her that
made him want to sleep alone, respect for her self-
consciousness about her mutilated body, her temporary
need for privacy, even from him? Or was it his own aver-
sion, his own embarrassment, that made him stay away?
How long had it been since they'd made love? What
inhibitions, fears, resentments, would they both now have
to overcome to reestablish their old intimacy, to delight
again in one another? How much pain would overcoming them involve?

My mother, too, would be awaiting Beth. She
hadn't called at all since dropping Gabbi off on Sunday.
"I don't want to bother her," is all she'd say when I'd ask
her why. Though angry over what had happened, angry
and I think humiliated by what the incident revealed
about her as her daughter's mother, nevertheless she'd be
the first to call once Beth was home, her voice perhaps
maintaining a civility too chiseled not to show how

wounded she still felt. That chilliness would pass eventually, as it always had before, and sooner or later, till the next fight, my mother would be able to cling again to her most cherished hope, that just as she had been the best of daughters to her own mother, so too, with Beth, she was the best of mothers; that the two of them, in spite of everything, were the closest of friends, like sisters.

In 1973, I worked as a night watchman for a consulting firm in Cambridge, Massachusetts. I worked from ten P.M. till six A.M. In the early hours, as I did my rounds, in order to keep myself awake I acquired the peculiar habit of composing eulogies out loud for all my living friends and relatives. It was a heady, morbid, entertaining exercise, to think about the lives of those I loved as fixed, as finished, to imagine myself at the memorial service, stern judge and forgiving advocate, with generosity and insight offering the final word on the totality of who I thought these people were. It was as if the only way that I could think about them clearly was to think about them gone. Imagining them dead I wrestled into focus, or thought I did, the protean feints and dodges of their very being.

My grandmother inspired the most elaborate eulogies. By then I hardly ever saw her. Our intimacy had long since disappeared. As I entered my teens, I too became embarrassed by her paranoid hallucinations, her weeping fits, her abrasive shifts in mood, her obesity, her tottering gait, her accidents, the smothering perfume she wore to hide the smell. When I was fifteen, she fell one night outside the bathroom, fracturing her arm and cheekbone. From that time on, she went from nursing home to nursing home as her condition worsened. And the more my mother nagged me to go visit, the more I stubbornly resisted. However much I avoided her by then, in the wee hours of my shift I was still the loving and devoted grandson, waxing eloquent about her daily struggle to preserve her dignity against the degradation of her body. As I eulogized her life, I suddenly could see so sharply what probably would have eluded me had I thought of her as still alive—how intimately connected were her strengths and weaknesses, how the indomitable will that had enabled her to thrive in business at a time when few women did became embittered willfulness when she got sick and had to live with us. I could see the misery behind the lashing cruelty, the desperate pride behind the spiky temper. I forgave her for the fights my

parents had on her account, for the humiliation I would
feel when my friends and I would see her in the street,
baby-stepping her enormous body to the beauty parlor,
panting "*Oy Gottenyu, Oy Gottenyu*." I forgave her for
that humiliation, and I forgave myself for feeling it. Most
of all I forgave her for what her body in all its terrifying
accidents and changes had robbed my childhood of—the
feeling that I would never die; that the body was something to be counted on, trusted; that change could only
mean addition not subtraction, opportunity not danger.

And then there was my sister. There were no eulogies for her then. A few years after my grandmother
came to live with us and my sister went away to college,
my parents disowned her when they discovered she was
living with a black man. "Shacking up with *shvartzers*" is
how they used to put it. Only many years later, after she
married Russ, a black man, and Gabbi was born, did my
parents finally overcome their prejudice enough to recon-
cile with Beth, the three of them establishing an often
strained but up to now resilient truce. In any event, for
all intents and purposes, throughout my adolescence
Beth was dead to me, only coming back to life a few
years later when I moved away from home and she and I

began to visit one another. During her isolation we spent more time together than we had since childhood. I got to know her far more intimately than I ever had before as I watched her struggle (like Nana) not just to survive, but to preserve or discover within such terrible circumstances whatever dignity she could. In a sense Beth seemed most alive, most fully and irreplaceably there before me, during the very period when her life was most imperiled. If she had been too absent from my life for me to eulogize her twenty years before, now she was too present. The last thing in the world I wanted was to sum her up, to think about her life as over.

POSTSCRIPT

I initially conceived this project as a personal testimony
to the power of poetry to alter how we live. Imagining
each essay as flowing out of and meditatively returning to
those moments in which certain poems take on a second
life in memory, fusing with the life they mirror, I wanted
to celebrate the transformative energies that poems can
engage. Now that the book is completed, what I'm left
with is a painfully immediate knowledge of the limits of
that transformative power.

My sister died on August 3, 1995, five weeks after

this manuscript was completed. Throughout the spring she'd been complaining of sinus headaches, and she was told in May that the cancer had spread to her brain and was inoperable. Her oncologist said that she had six months at the most to live. In June, however, she deteriorated rapidly. She was hospitalized at the beginning of July, and, as I had the year before, I flew in to be with her.

As I sat beside Beth for those last four weeks, first at the hospital, then at the hospice, I was too deep inside the necessity of tending her, of grieving for her, to think of any poem that might console or clarify. In fact, the idea of consolation or clarity seemed abhorrent, a betrayal of the devastating privilege of this most intimate and personal experience. To write in detail about it now would also feel like a betrayal, not because I couldn't find a language capable of doing justice to what I've just been through, but rather because to write about my sister's death, even to tell (as I have) bits and pieces of the story to friends and family, is to stand outside it, and therefore to transform my sister from the inchoate immediacy of feeling, where she's still so present to me, into the realm of public discourse, where she'd inevitably become a "subject" of an essay, or a conversation, or a poem, a "subject" whose significance and clarity is gained through the perspective that only separation, only distance, can bestow.

Beth's death is unacceptable to me. Unfair. Unjust. And yet my sense of unredeemable loss is all I have of her. It's where she lives most vividly. Acceptance, I know, will come. And with acceptance, also the desire to give a public shape, texture, understanding, and significance to who she was, what she went through, what she meant to me. Some day I may write in more detail about my sister. But not today.

Notes

page 1 Eugenio Montale, *The Second Life of Art* (New York: Ecco, 1982), 21.

page 4 Elizabeth Bishop, *The Complete Poems 1927–1979* (New York: Farrar Straus Giroux, 1983), 64.

page 6 T. S. Eliot, *Selected Essays* (New York: Harcourt Brace & Co., 1950), 5.

page 13 Mircea Eliade, *The Sacred and the Profane* (New York: Harcourt Brace, 1959), 92. Also see *The Myth of the Eternal Return* (New Jersey: Princeton, 1974), 76.

page 24 Philip Larkin, *Collected Poems* (New York: Farrar Straus Giroux, 1989), 97.

page 44 Godfrey Hodgson, *America in Our Time* (New York: Vintage, 1976), 308–9.

page 50 Lyrics from "Mr. Tambourine Man," by Bob Dylan, copyright 1964 Warner Bros. Inc.

page 54 Charles Taylor, *Sources of the Self* (Cambridge: Harvard, 1989), 152.

page 54   Robert Stephen Spitz, *Barefoot in Babylon: The Creation of the Woodstock Music Festival, 1969* (New York: Viking, 1979), 37–38.

page 58   Thom Gunn, *The Occasions of Poetry* (London: Faber & Faber, 1982), 182.

page 60   Thom Gunn, *Collected Poems* (New York: Farrar Straus Giroux, 1994), 239.

page 61   John Keats, *Selected Poems and Letters* (Boston: Houghton Mifflin, 1959), 253.

page 71   Larkin, *Collected Poems,* 165.

page 78   Charles Baudelaire, *Flowers of Evil* (New York: New Directions, 1962), 121.

page 87   W. H. Auden, *Selected Poems* (London: Faber, 1968), 40.

page 88   Christopher Marlowe, "The Passionate Shepherd to His Love."

page 90   W. B. Yeats, *The Poems of W. B. Yeats* (New York: Macmillan, 1983), 345.

page 106   Thomas Hardy, *Selected Shorter Poems* (London: Macmillan, 1972), 81.

page 108   Seamus Heaney, *Poems 1965–1975* (New York: Farrar Straus Giroux, 1980), 170.

page 134   Yvor Winters, *Collected Poems* (Chicago: Swallow), 120.

page 136   For the Gershom Scholem quote see Liz Harris, *Holy Days* (New York: Collier, 1985), 80.

page 139   Montaigne, *The Complete Essays of Montaigne* (Palo Alto: Stanford University Press, 1958), 856.

page 143   Yvor Winters, *Collected Poems,* 73.

page 145   William Wordsworth, *The Prelude* (New York: Rinehart & Co., 1954), 430.

page 149   Elizabeth Bishop, *The Complete Poems,* 20.

page 154   E. A. Robinson, *Selected Poems of E. A. Robinson* (New York: Collier, 1976), 209.

page 154   Robert Frost, *The Poetry of Robert Frost* (New York: Holt Rinehart, 1974), 245.

page 154   Emily Dickinson, *Selected Poems & Letters of Emily Dickinson* (New York: Doubleday, 1959), 77.

page 154   Thomas Hardy, *Selected Shorter Poems,* 23.

page 156   Aristotle, *Nicomachean Ethics,* book 8.I.

page 161   Wayne Booth, *The Company We Keep* (Berkeley: University of California Press, 1988), 254.

page 163   See *The Odyssey,* trans. Richmond Lattimore (New York: Harper & Row, 1967), 123 (book 8, lines 71–82).

page 163   Bertolt Brecht, *The Threepenny Opera.*

page 169   Simone Weil, *Gravity and Grace* (London: Routledge, 1972), 132.

page 171   Janet Lewis, *Poems Old and New 1918–1978* (Athens: Swallow, 1981), 68.

page 174   Elizabeth Bishop, *The Complete Poems,* 169.

page 176   D. R. MacDonald, *Eyestone* (New York: Norton, 1987), 91.

page 190   G. K. Chesterton, *Heretics* (Freeport: Books for Libraries Press, 1970), 189.

page 210   Robert Frost, *The Poetry of Robert Frost,* 136.

page 214   John Keats, *Selected Poems and Letters,* 253.